Future Proofing

David Birchall and George Tovstiga

■ Fast track route to understanding and managing your business future.

■ Covers all the key aspects of future proofing, from identifying alternative scenarios and tracking technology change to developing a blueprint for action and communicating it within the organization

■ Examples and lessons from benchmark businesses, including ABB, Shell and Anglo American, and ideas from the smartest thinkers including Gary Hamel, Peter Senge and Chris Argyris

■ Includes a glossary of key concepts and a comprehensive resources guide

>>EXPRESS EXEC.COM<<
essential management thinking at your fingertips

Copyright © Capstone Publishing 2002

The right of David Birchall and George Tovstiga to be identified as the authors of this work has been asserted in accordance with the Copyright, Designs and Patents Act 1988

First published 2002 by
Capstone Publishing (a Wiley company)
8 Newtec Place
Magdalen Road
Oxford OX4 1RE
United Kingdom
http://www.capstoneideas.com

All rights reserved. Except for the quotation of short passages for the purposes of criticism and review, no part of this publication may be reproduced, stored in a retrieval system, or transmitted, in any form or by any means, electronic, mechanical, photocopying, recording or otherwise, without the prior permission of the publisher.

CIP catalogue records for this book are available from the British Library and the US Library of Congress

ISBN 1-84112-327-7

This book is printed on acid-free paper

Substantial discounts on bulk quantities of Capstone books are available to corporations, professional associations and other organizations. Please contact Capstone for more details on +44 (0)1865 798 623 or (fax) +44 (0)1865 240 941 or (e-mail) info@wiley-capstone.co.uk

Contents

Introduction to ExpressExec

ExpressExec is 3 million words of the latest management thinking compiled into 10 modules. Each module contains 10 individual titles forming a comprehensive resource of current business practice written by leading practitioners in their field. From brand management to balanced scorecard, ExpressExec enables you to grasp the key concepts behind each subject and implement the theory immediately. Each of the 100 titles is available in print and electronic formats.

Through the ExpressExec.com Website you will discover that you can access the complete resource in a number of ways:

» printed books or e-books;
» e-content – PDF or XML (for licensed syndication) adding value to an intranet or Internet site;
» a corporate e-learning/knowledge management solution providing a cost-effective platform for developing skills and sharing knowledge within an organization;
» bespoke delivery – tailored solutions to solve your need.

Why not visit www.expressexec.com and register for free key management briefings, a monthly newsletter and interactive skills checklists. Share your ideas about ExpressExec and your thoughts about business today.

Please contact elound@wiley-capstone.co.uk for more information.

Introduction to Future Proofing

The first chapter explains why future proofing is so important to managers in the twenty-first century.

Manufacturers and service providers are constantly using new technologies both to upgrade their products and services and to create new and radical alternatives to those offered by other companies. But for both business and consumers, any attempt to keep up can be very expensive. It is already clear that in many fields of activity the rules of the game are changing. Customers are showing strong resistance to constant replacement in order to get only marginal improvements in usability, and many producers are reconfiguring their offerings to refocus their value-adding away from basic hardware or software to customer solutions.

So if I bought a new car it would be very attractive if I knew that either my dashboard or my windscreen would be changed easily at regular intervals to accommodate new information and communications systems, such as the latest technology traffic information, personalized entertainment, or voice-activated e-mail. My car might well have a somewhat old, classic shell, still be in excellent working order and general condition, but at relatively low cost would have state-of-the-art electronics. Or if, say, I operated a supermarket chain with large refrigeration units, it would be ideal if, when functionality was available, simple modification was possible – a "plug and play" principle – rather than complete replacement.

This is a principle already applied in the computer industry where, within limits, upgrades to software can be added easily to existing system configurations. Across an increasing spectrum, the initial purchase decision is being very much influenced by considerations of lifetime costs and by perceptions of the impact of future developments on potential obsolescence. Manufacturers are having to respond as sustainability becomes an increasingly important consideration, and are having to find alternative sources of added value – their proposition to the customer is fast becoming one of *future proofing*, guaranteeing upgrades at low costs and with minimal disruption to service.

Faced with an uncertain future, it would be attractive if one could apply similar principles to organizations. In order to better prepare for the future, if organizations can understand those areas most likely to be subject to rapid or disruptive change, and those areas which are more constant, and then create appropriate levels of flexibility and adaptability, they can be in better shape and more prepared to seize opportunities.

Just as in the examples of software artefacts, the creation of a new model for operations is essential. The starting point for this is forward thinking, and a high degree of foresight. The vision of what the organization is aiming to be is essential. Creating possible scenarios for the environment in which the organization might be operating enables the testing of plans and an assessment of their adequacy. A clear understanding of changes provides the backcloth, integrating an understanding of technology development and its potential impact, patterns of customer wants and needs, the labour market, the competitive landscape, the political climate, legislative and fiscal, and the internal capabilities which can be deployed to exploit this "future."

Many business executives find it difficult to free up time for a systematic look forward, particularly those running small and medium-sized businesses. This book sets out to help executives and senior managers, whatever their business, who want to prepare their organizations and themselves for the future. It presents an overall approach which has been demonstrated to help executives in strategic decision making. It explains the common tools and techniques which are available to assist in the process. Completing the process will result in a clear identification of capabilities essential to underpin the chosen future direction.

An Introduction to the Concepts

This chapter introduces key terms and concepts that are relevant to the notion of future proofing.

In this section we will define a number of key terms and concepts that are relevant to the notion of "future proofing." The picture we will use to position these terms and concepts is shown in Fig. 1.1. "Future proofing" requires that firms understand (1) where they stand today, competitively speaking, and (2) how to develop the means to build a viable vision of, and map to, the firm of the future. These terms and concepts constitute important building blocks for future proofing.

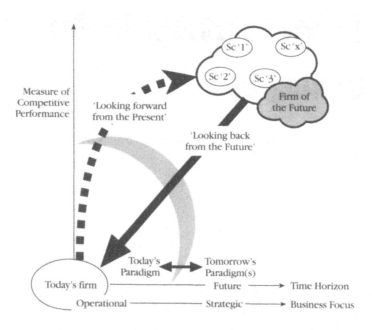

Fig. 2.1 Creating the vision of the firm of the future.

FUTURE PROOFING

Future proofing is an approach to structuring collective thinking in order to better understand the essentials of business futures to enable organizations to respond in the most effective way. It recognizes that there is no "one solution" but that organizations need to have a strong vision and flexible routes to achieving that vision. Some elements in the pathway will be more predictable than others, but by understanding those areas where the organization is most at risk, early warning signals of deviation can be detected and plans established to take advantage of new opportunities.

Future proofing is a concept borrowed from the field of technology management, where organizations seek to minimize the risks of investing in technologies which soon become obsolete and are then prohibitively expensive to replace. The overall aim is to ensure that future obsolescence is minimized by designing facilities or equipment so that they are flexible and open-ended enough to allow for growth, are attentive to the changing needs of users, and yet are affordable. There is always a trade-off in cost between design "fit for purpose" and building into design "flexibility" and "adaptability." For organizations, well-developed foresight can enable informed strategic formulation and more effective development and deployment of resources so as to meet a range of possible futures. A better balance can be struck between "lean" and "flexible" operations, focusing more on the longer term rather than immediate goal attainment. In seeking to establish those areas "at risk" to rapid change, strategies can be developed to minimize expensive redundancy.

By focusing on the development of technology platforms rather than single, unconnected technologies, organizations can build greater product and services endurance. But probably of greater lasting impact is a strong business platform, which embraces product and service with high-level intangibles such as brand and customer loyalty. However, no organization is immune from attack by disruptive products and services based on a leap forward in technology applications.

SCENARIOS

Scenarios are "tools for foresight discussions and documents whose purpose is not a prediction or a plan but a change in the mindset of the people who use them."

De Geus (1997) The Living Company, p. 46

Scenario literally means the written version of a play or story. Business scenarios are "focused descriptions of fundamentally different futures presented in coherent script-like or narrative fashion."[1] Scenarios are plausible and challenging stories, not forecasts. They do not extrapolate from the past to predict what will happen in the future, but instead offer several very different stories of how the future might look. They are used by organizations in preparing themselves for discontinuities and sudden change. They can be used to create a common culture or language through which the future can be imagined and discussed. They also challenge the "mental models" commonly held by members of organizations. Their use can underpin organizational learning.

FORESIGHT

Foresight programs bring together experts from a wide range of backgrounds to build common perceptions of long-term trends in order to identify areas of strategic research and the emerging generic technologies likely to yield the greatest economic and social welfare. While early government-sponsored Foresights were mainly concerned with technological developments, a recognition of the interactions between technological developments, social, and cultural circumstances has led to a broadening of Foresight to areas such as the ageing population, crime prevention and sustainability, as well as the broadening of technology-related fields to include societal impact.[2]

Foresight does not claim to predict a certain future situation but rather recognizes that a range of possibilities exists; it attempts to shape or create paths for development. Results are widely disseminated to inform policy makers, whether in government or industry.

COMPETENCIES

Competencies are manifestations of organizational knowledge in the firm. They are the basis for competitive differentiation. We distinguish at three levels of the organization: individual competencies, group or team-based competencies (which we will refer to as capabilities), and core competencies, which are competencies at the corporate or firm level.

Individual competencies have been defined as people's underlying characteristics and indicate the way in which they behave, think, and generalize across situations. They represent a personal embodiment of knowledge and skills accumulated over time through training and experience.

Capabilities are competencies at the team or group level. These are clusters of skill sets representing the collective knowledge, skills, and experience in a team. Harvard Business School Professor Dorothy Leonard-Barton[3] has suggested that capabilities may be broken down into at least four interdependent dimensions, two of which are knowledge competence repositories.

1 People-embodied knowledge and skills.
2 Physical technical systems, two of which are organizational knowledge control and channeling mechanisms.
3 Managerial systems.
4 Organizational culture, values, and norms.

Finally, core competencies are bundles of constituent capabilities and technologies that create disproportionate value for the customer, differentiating their owner from the competitors and allowing entrance to new markets, as explained by London Business School's Professor Gary Hamel.[4] Competencies are not assets in the conventional accounting sense of the word; they are intangible features which represent an accumulation of learning over time. Firms face the challenge of managing their current portfolio of competencies today while acquiring and developing new capabilities that will be required tomorrow.

> Honda's ability to produce some of the world's best engines and power trains is one of its core competencies. This ability provides Honda's customers with highly valued benefits such as superior fuel economy, zippy acceleration, easy revving, and less noise and vibration.

TECHNOLOGY ROADMAPPING

Technology roadmapping is used at both industry and firm level. By bringing together the world's leading expertise, industry-level exercises gain an understanding of the direction in which technology is likely to develop and the anticipated timescales. It then serves to assist universities, funding agencies, trade bodies, and firms in setting the research and development (R&D) agenda. It gives the industry overall a common reference and encourages co-operative investment and a more uniform sharing of the R&D costs. To be useful, such roadmaps must include action items which "galvanize" the industry towards the roadmap's stated goals. The industry roadmap can serve to inform roadmapping at the level of the individual firm.

At a firm level, the overarching aim of roadmapping is to achieve improved time to market, and thereby a strengthened competitive position. In order to improve the product creation process, a long-term view of technology and market developments improves planning. It is being used to achieve better integration between the overall business strategy and its technology strategy. Having an agreed overall plan can also support people at all levels in achieving milestones, and can lead to greater commitment to their role in the overall process.

To be effective as a communications tool the roadmaps should identify links between technologies, sub-systems, and their interfaces to form a coherent technology platform which may well apply over different product groups.

QUALITY FUNCTION DEPLOYMENT

Quality function deployment (QFD) was developed as a tool to support the conversion of customer demands into quality characteristics which then form the basis of a quality plan for the finished products or services. The characteristics and customer desires are often weighted in importance to help identify priorities, a feature of the QFD process which is seen as particularly valuable. Competitive benchmarking is used to inform the setting of target values. The charts also serve to map out what are complex, inter-related sets of inputs and outputs. But unless "exciting" customer needs are identified, the product development is unlikely to "break the mold."

Not only are such techniques used in manufacturing, they are also found in software development, service and process improvement, and research portfolio analysis. They are particularly useful where concurrent engineering is being deployed to cut down time from concept to market. They can serve to inform technology roadmapping and are most useful at a preliminary stage. The original concept of QFD can be extended beyond the rather limited basic functionality of the product or service to include the wider range of intangibles such as aesthetic qualities and image.

KNOWLEDGE, INTELLECTUAL CAPITAL, AND KNOWLEDGE MANAGEMENT

As knowledge is increasingly becoming the primary factor of competitiveness, replacing traditional factors such as land, labour, and capital, future proofing will demand that firms succeed in identifying, leveraging, and exploiting their knowledge assets.

Knowledge is the integration of information, ideas, experience, intuition, skill, and lessons learned that can create added value for a business, its employees, its products, its services, and its customers. *Explicit* knowledge includes the content of books, manuals, and reports. It is easily identifiable and simple to articulate and communicate. However, much of the strategically relevant knowledge in organizations is *tacit* – it resides in people's heads and includes intuition, insight, perception, feelings, and personal beliefs. By definition, it is elusive, being difficult both to capture and to communicate. It is the cumulative set of beliefs, insights, experiences, and procedures that guide people's thoughts, behaviour, and communication.

Intellectual capital has been used to describe intangible assets derived from knowledge which contribute to wealth creation. Intellectual capital can be based on human, organizational, or customer capital. *Human capital*, for example, relates to the ability of individuals or teams to apply creative solutions to customers' needs. *Organizational capital* relates to the collective knowledge of the organization, tacit and codified – knowledge embedded in knowledge databases, business processes, the technology infrastructure, and the culture of the organization. *Customer capital* reflects the strength of the firm's relationship with its customers, superior customer-perceived value, and increasing customization of business solutions. Finally, *intellectual capital* can be said to be the relationship between human, organizational, and customer capital that maximizes the creation of customer value, leading ultimately to the creation of some form of wealth.[5]

Knowledge management has been defined to be a conscious effort on the part of the organization of getting the right knowledge to the right people at the right time, and helping and encouraging people to share knowledge in ways that strive to improve organizational performance.[6] Whether or not knowledge can be "managed" at all is still a topic of debate. Knowledge "management" should be viewed as the effort on the part of the organization to create the requisite *enabling conditions* for the free flow and exchange of strategically relevant knowledge between people.[7]

> Knowledge management begins with "knowing what the organization knows." Lew Platt, former CEO of Hewlett-Packard, is credited with saying: "If HP knew what HP knows, we would be three times as profitable."[8]

ORGANIZATIONAL LEARNING

Peter Senge, director of the Center for Organization Learning at MIT's Sloan School of Management, in writing in *The Fifth Discipline*[9] did much to establish the concept of the learning organization, stating his belief that the essence of the learning organization is based upon five disciplines.

1 *Personal mastery* – essentially enabling people to develop themselves towards the goals and purposes that they choose for themselves.
2 *Mental models* – checking constantly that our internal view of the world matches with the realities we observe and that we act in line with these models.
3 *Shared vision* – being a member of a group that shares images of the future and explores ways of getting there.
4 *Team learning* – through sharing and discussion, enabling all team members to develop collective intelligence which is in excess of the sum of each individual's capabilities.
5 *Systems thinking* – looking at systems in a holistic manner and looking for inter-relationships between components.

Arie De Geus, who for many years worked in Shell International, makes an important point about learning taking place in any decision-making process, but one key point about the learning organization is that it is seeking not only to accelerate that learning but also to make sure that it is "deep learning."[10]

> "However, even if our meetings are not well organized they are still conducted through conversation. The process of conversation goes through four stages ... As it happens, these four elements – perceiving, embedding, concluding, and acting – are seen by various psychologists as the defining elements of learning. Whether they are managed effectively or not doesn't matter. Every act of decision making is a learning process."
> De Geus *(1997) The Living Company, pp. 73–4*

Chris Argyris, working out of Harvard Business School, and Donald Schon, from the Massachusetts Institute of Technology, made a significant contribution to the foundation of the concept of organizational learning. They adopted the notion of agency theory to explain the important and conceptually difficult link between individual and organizational learning:

> "Organizational learning occurs when individuals within an organization experience a problematic situation and inquire into it on the organization's behalf. They experience a surprising mismatch between expected and actual results of action and respond to that mismatch through a process of thought and further action that leads them to modify their images of organization or their understandings of organizational phenomena, and to restructure their activities so as to bring outcomes and expectations into line, thereby changing organizational theory-in-use. In order to become organizational, the learning that results from organizational inquiry must become embedded in the images of organization held in its members' minds and/or the epistemological artefacts (the maps, memories, and programs) embedded in the organizational environment." (p16)[11]

VALUE PROPOSITION

A value proposition is a business case for action; it is the logical link between action and payoff. The firm's value proposition is an articulation of its unique business rationale – its justification for existing in its business environment; its business *raison d'être* so to speak. It is an articulation of how the firm intends to position itself relative to its competitors; what differential value offering it proposes to offer its customers.

The firm's value proposition is based on a number of assumptions the firm makes and continually scrutinizes for validity and adjustment. Management guru Peter Drucker[12] points out that these assumptions ultimately shape the organization's behaviour, dictate its decisions about what to do, and establish what the organization defines as meaningful results. Drucker refers to three specific assumptions that are relevant for the firm's value proposition.

1 There are the assumptions about the competitive *environment* of the firm: the society and its structure, political trends and developments, the markets, the customers, the competitors, and technology.
2 There are the assumptions about the firm's *mission and vision*.
3 There are the assumptions about the *core competencies* needed by the firm to succeed in its environment and to accomplish its mission. These define the areas in which an organization must excel in order to maintain leadership.

Together, these assumptions form the basis of the firm's value proposition, which is its implicit promise to its customers with respect to its *differential value* offering – its particular combination of values: price, quality, performance, convenience, selection, etc.[13]

Nokia's phenomenal rise to become one of Europe's hottest technology companies is in no small way tied to its value proposition. This is based on a deeply held belief shared throughout the company that the devices it is making satisfy a basic human need to communicate. "Nokians" see them helping to create a new world, which they call the "mobile information society."

World-class capabilities in branding, logistics, and manufacturing have enabled Nokia to deliver on this value proposition with a remarkable degree of success.[14]

TECHNOLOGICAL DISCONTINUITIES AND DISRUPTIVE TECHNOLOGIES

An important part of future proofing involves dealing effectively with technological discontinuities. These are radical, generally unpredictable innovations which enable the emergence of order-of-magnitude changes in technology which in turn enable fundamentally different product and/or service offerings and process design.[15] Product discontinuities are fundamentally different product forms that command a clearly differentiated price, performance, or quality advantage over previous products. Process discontinuities involve fundamentally different ways of making a product or service. These are reflected in quantum improvements in quality, cost, and access to new markets.

Technological discontinuities can occur in any industry sector. Examples include digital mobile telephony, high-performance polymers, mini-mill steel making, biotechnology, genetic engineering, and computer optical storage systems. All of these are changing the world we live in, in some way or another. They have created new business opportunities for some companies and have put others out of business.

Technological discontinuities are brought on by the emergence of disruptive technologies.[16] These typically have worse performance than the current technologies in use, at least in the near term. They have design features which initially are valued by only a few fringe and generally new customers. These features, however, often represent a key source of competitive advantage in the future. Furthermore, products based on disruptive technologies are often cheaper, simpler, smaller, and typically more convenient to use. Finally, disruptive technologies often bring in a new and different value proposition.

As far as disruptive technologies go, e-commerce has set precedents. The impact of disruptive technologies has been felt particularly pervasively in retailing, where discounters have seized dominance from traditional retailers and variety stores, thereby virtually disrupting all previous retailing models. Charles Schwab was a disrupter to the Merrill Lynches of the world. Now E-Trade is coming up on the market from below. Numerous other lower-cost service providers are crowding in.

GAPS AND GAP ANALYSIS

Future proofing ultimately requires that opportunity and performance gaps be identified and closed. Gaps represent differences between desired (future) and actual (current) competitive performance. They represent the difference between what the firm believes it *must do* (strategic intent) and what the firm *can do* (firm's current reality); between what the firm *must know* and what the firm, in fact, *does know*.

As suggested in Fig. 2.2, the firm can be shown to have at any point in time a strategic gap as well as a knowledge gap. These represent the difference between the collective aspirations of the organization with respect to what it must do and must know, articulated by its value proposition, and its current reality, reflected by what it can do and does know. Gaps reflect and determine the firm's competitive limitations, and show where the firm needs to improve (that is, close the gap). Inevitably, gaps represent organizational change, but also opportunities for improvement. Change options can be derived from the outcomes of analyzing the two gaps.

Strategic and knowledge gaps can be identified and analyzed with the help of specific methods and tools that provide a reliable picture of the firm's current competitive position. This may be a strategic portfolio analysis methodology, such as the one developed by the authors in a recent research project (2000),[17] which results in a visual mapping of the firm's capabilities in terms of their competitive impact and strength. The analysis shows where strategic knowledge gaps exist in the firm's portfolio, indicating areas in which it must invest resources in order to build a position of future competitiveness.

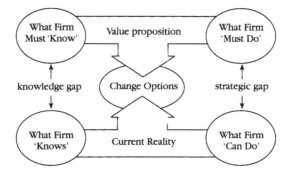

Fig. 2.2 Strategic gaps and knowledge gaps: options for organizational change. (Based on Zack, M. (1999) "Developing a knowledge strategy," *California Management Review*, spring issue.)

TRENDS ANALYSIS

Trends analysis is an important tool for future proofing. Trends analysis and competitive intelligence are strategic exercises that seek to support and extend the firm's planning horizon into the future. The horizon can be perhaps two, five, or more years, depending on the business involved. The questions typically asked are: What trends will mature or emerge by that time? What will be the driving forces of the market? What will be the key success factors of the market? What new technologies might emerge that could prove to be disruptive and discontinuous? Who will the competitors be? What will the firm need in terms of capabilities and competencies to build a position of competitive advantage in the future?

In order to provide answers to these questions, managers must grasp a highly complex set of interacting factors. They must understand the industry's history, time frames and structure, and stakeholders. The organization must also be clear about its own scope of competition. It must be capable of analyzing the external forces that shape its day-to-day operations and its strategic thrust. These may be grouped into five categories: economic, political, societal, technological, and industry. For each, key trends are established and analyzed according to impact. The impact can be positive, neutral (indeterminate), or negative. The impact analysis provides a good opportunity for cross-checking key success factors determined in the analysis described in the previous section. Table 2.1 suggests a framework for examining trends and deriving the strategic impact for the firm.

Table 2.1 A framework for examining trends and deriving the strategic impact for the firm.

Time frame and scope	Trends and uncertainties	Impact on firm
1 What is the firm's TIME FRAME?	1 ECONOMIC	
» Pace of technological development?	» Shift toward network-knowledge economy?	
» Competitors' time frame?	» Impact of globalization?	
» Investment intensity?	2 POLITICAL	
» Political time frame?	» Selective trade barriers/agreements?	Positive
2 What is the firm's SCOPE?	» Legislation? Deregulation?	Neutral?
» Domestic versus global?	» North-south/east-west migration?	Negative?
3 Who are the STAKEHOLDERS?	3 SOCIETAL	
» Clients/shareholders/employees?	» Increase in environmental sensitivity?	
» Investors/society at large?	4 TECHNOLOGICAL	
	» Potential technological discontinuities?	
	5 INDUSTRY	
	» Shifts; emergence of new industries?	

CHANGE PATH

Change path refers to the mode of improvement a firm chooses in order to bridge the gap of competitive performance between its competitive position today and the future state it envisions for itself (see Fig. 2.3). Different competitive situations and demands require different paths of change. Successful change takes place on a pathway that is appropriate to the specific needs of the firm. Indeed, the pathways may be quite different. Change may proceed along a radical path or it may involve incremental, step-wise adaptation.

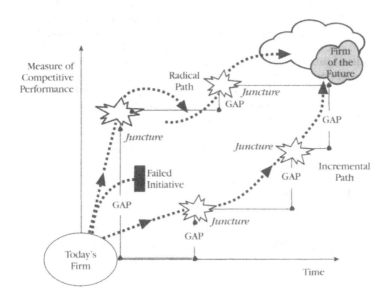

Fig. 2.3 Plotting the path of change – radical versus incremental approaches.

Common to both pathways are "junctures," critical points along a pathway of change at which one or more critical issues need to be resolved. Junctures typically involve organizational issues such as structure, human resources, culture, or processes. Failure to resolve a juncture inevitably results in a breakdown of the change initiative at that point along the pathway.

Radical change characteristically features one or more discontinuities along its trajectory. Discontinuities represent the firm's response to revolutionary change in its competitive environments. Alternatively, it could be the firm's response to dealing with disruptive innovation. Disruptive innovations create entirely new markets that move away from existing mainstream markets. Radical change may require "jumping the curve" one or more times. Incremental change, following a gradual, incremental path, is often of the reactive type. Change of this sort is often adaptive in nature and its scope is typically limited to parts of the firm. The pace is also often sporadic. Just as in the case of radical change, however, junctures along the incremental path need to be appropriately addressed and resolved.

In reality, change in organizations is probably a combination of both types. Change management thinkers Tushman *et al*[18] and Tushman and O'Reilly[19] describe change in innovative organizations as often being a combination of long periods of incremental change punctuated by discontinuous, frame-breaking, organizational change.

RISK ASSESSMENT AND PORTFOLIO MANAGEMENT

Through future proofing organizations identify their long-term vision and then plan a direction which reduces the risks of failed investment while being flexible enough to accommodate the unexpected. Techniques such as technology roadmapping can be the basis of decision making about how the business will access the new technologies that it needs to secure its desired future. The result of such exercises will be a portfolio of technology needs.

The firm is then faced with strategic decisions about how best to acquire the level of access and control it deems necessary to support its future product or service portfolio. Decisions have to be taken about how to allocate R&D budgets, including investment in internal R&D as well as in work done by partners such as universities and other technology companies. In determining such decisions a view has to be taken on how best to manage risk. This needs to be based on an understanding of the risks involved in each potential project within the portfolio and also the risk across the portfolio.

One aspect of this is the establishment of technology platforms – described by Marc Meyer, an authority in the field and a specialist in technology management from North Eastern University, along with his co-author Paul Mugge, from IBM's Consulting Practice, as "simple pictures of major subsystems and interfaces between these subsystems, simple descriptions of the purpose and technologies within subsystems and interfaces, and a clear articulation about how the common subsystems can be leveraged into different product groups."[20] This can then enable a more effective assessment of the likely impact of technological change.

Another important consideration is the balancing of the portfolio so that new products/services start to generate income before old products reach the end of their life cycle, and product/services are not all subject to the same influences in economic cycles. While methodologies exist for risk assessment, they all have weaknesses, and like many other approaches, in practice executives have to use "gut feel" alongside the results of analytical methods. But in order to arrive at the best possible outcomes, a decision and review structure is important – a review committee which is well constituted and willing to take tough decisions to ensure progress in line with strategic intent.

NOTES

1 Schoemaker, P. (1993) "Multiple scenario development: its conceptual and behavioural," *Strategic Management Journal*, **14** (3), p. 193.

2 http://.www.foresight.gov.uk

3 Leonard-Barton, D. (1995) *Wellsprings of Knowledge*, Harvard Business School Press, Boston.

4 Hamel, G. (1994) "The concept of core competence," in *Competence-Based Competition* (eds Hamel, G. & Heene, A.), John Wiley & Sons Ltd, Chichester.

5 Bukowitz, W.R & Williams, R.L. (1999) *The Knowledge Management Fieldbook*, Financial Times Prentice Hall, London.

6 O'Dell, C. & Grayson, C.J. (1998) *If Only We Knew What We Know*, Free Press, New York.

7 von Krogh, G., Ichijo, K. & Nonaka, I. (2000) *Enabling Knowledge Creation*, Oxford University Press, Oxford.

8 Despres, Charles & Chauvel, Daniele (1999) "How to map knowledge management," *Financial Times*, March 7, (*FT Mastering Information Management*, Part Six, Knowledge Management).

9 Senge, P.M. (1990) *The Fifth Discipline – The Art and Practice of the Learning Organization*, Doubleday/Currency, London.

10 de Geus, A. (1997) *The Living Company*, Nicholas Brealey Publishing, London.

11 Argyris, C. & Schon, D. (1978) *Organizational Learning*, Addison-Wesley, Reading, MA.

12 Drucker P.F. (1994) "The theory of business," *Harvard Business Review*, **72** (5), p. 95.

13 Treacy, M. & Wiersema, F. (1995) *The Discipline of Market Leaders*, Addison-Wesley Publishing Company, London.

14 Guyon, J. (1999) "Next up for cell phones: weaving a wireless web," *Fortune*, October 25, **140** (8), p. 224.

15 Tushman, M.L. & Rosenkopf, L. (1996) "Organizational determinants of technological change: toward a sociology of technological evolution," in *Strategic Management of Technology and Innovation*, 2nd edn (eds Burgelman, R.A., Maidique, M.A. & Wheelwright, S.C.), Irwin.

16 Christensen, C.M. (1997) *The Innovator's Dilemma*, Harvard Business School Press, Boston. See also Bower, J.L. & Christensen, C.M. (1995) "Disruptive technologies: catching the wave," *Harvard Business Review*, **73** (1), p. 43.

17 Birchall, D.W. & Tovstiga, G. (2001) "The strategic potential of a firm's knowledge portfolio," in *FT Handbook of Management*, 2nd edn (eds Crainer, S. & Dearlove, D.), Financial Times Prentice Hall, London.

18 Tushman, M.L., Anderson, P.C. & O'Reilly, C. (1997) "Technology cycles, innovation streams, and ambidextrous organizations: organization renewal through innovation streams and strategic change," in *Managing Strategic Innovation and Change* (eds Tushman, M. & Anderson, P.), Oxford University Press, New York.

19 Tushman, M.L. & O'Reilly, C.A. (1996) "Ambidextrous organizations: managing evolutionary and revolutionary change," *California Management Review*, **38** (4), pp. 8–30.

20 Meyer, M. & Mugge, P. (2001) "Make platform innovation drive enterprise growth," *Research Technology Management*, **44** (1), pp. 25–39.

The Evolution of Future Proofing

This chapter investigates a number of important conceptual approaches and practical frameworks that have evolved to support strategic decision-making processes that firms deploy in order to build future competitiveness.

Future proofing brings together ideas and concepts from many sources. It is part of a strategic process aimed at ensuring that decisions affecting the firm in the long term are made in the best-informed way. The process involves identifying those areas most at risk from rapid and even disruptive change, and preparing for such eventualities in forward planning. Scenario planning is probably the principal methodology underpinning future proofing and is certainly the starting point. But it is only the starting point for some tough decision making. Techniques such as Foresight, technology roadmapping, and quality function deployment are all useful, both at pre-scenario building and as the process of future proofing unfolds. An understanding of technological discontinuities is clearly important in preparing for the future and is a vital part of future proofing. But as importantly, for organizations to move forward effectively, organizational learning is a vital process.

SCENARIOS AND PLANNING

"Scenarios increase the organization's capability to more skilfully observe its environment, leading to more robust long-term organizational learning. It is seen as shifting strategic thinking from reactive to proactive and from internal to external."

Kees van der Heijden (1996) Scenarios – the Art of Strategic Conversation, Wiley, Chichester

Probably the first person to apply the term "scenario" to planning was the futurist Herman Kahn, a military strategist who used it in the early 1950s at the Rand Corporation.[1] He borrowed the term from the movie industry – "the sketch of the plot of a play; giving particulars of the scenes, situations, etc." He was best known for his scenarios about nuclear war, arguing that if people thought about the unthinkable they would be better prepared in the event of it happening. In the 1960s, an urban planning project in Paris used scenarios, but it was Shell's use of scenarios to predict and prepare for the 1973 oil crisis that is undoubtedly pre-eminent in all the reports of its use.[2] Above all, it demonstrated how the technique could be applied to gain considerable competitive advantage.

Scenarios, rather than being forecasts based on an extrapolation of past events and trends, are plausible and challenging stories depicting how the future might look. Scenarios assist in understanding complex situations and provide a useful tool for organizational learning. To have impact within organizations, scenarios have to be seen to be based on a holistic view of the complex interaction of environmental and internal variables, and written in a way that makes them seem plausible.[3]

There are at least three schools of scenario planning. The *intuitive school*, derived from Shell's experience, is largely qualitative, assuming that business decisions result from a process of finding and understanding complex inter-relationships between internal and external factors (including economic, political, technological, social, and environmental). The *quantitative school* uses operational research techniques such as econometric forecasting and time series. The third, a *hybrid school*, uses both intuitive and quantitative approaches. Computer-based systems such as groupware may be used to facilitate idea generation, perceptual mapping of factors and their impacts, and simulation software for testing scenarios.

Multiple scenarios are put together so that more than one future is considered. Having two is often seen as insufficient because they will be bipolar and leave little choice; having three is seen as leading to a middle road being chosen; but more than four often leads to too much overlap.

Scenario building normally involves a series of facilitated workshops. Elements typically included in this process are:

» reconsideration of vision and objectives;
» clarification of business ideas that will lead to success;
» identification of strategic priorities;
» identification of "gaps" between where the organization is now and where it would like to be in the future;
» identification of relevant actions to move the organization forward.

Paul Schoemaker, a leading consultant in the field as well as a professor at Wharton, outlines a ten-step process for scenario development.[4]

1 Define the time frame and scope of analysis (programs, products, technologies) and the knowledge that would be of greatest value to the organization.

2 Involve key stakeholders, including customers and suppliers, since scenarios are for strategy identification rather than strategy development.

3 Identify and briefly explain the basic trends, including how and why they exert influence on the organization.

4 Identify events with uncertain outcomes that will most likely affect the organization.

5 Construct initial scenario themes. Trends and uncertainties are the main ingredients for scenario development. Predetermined elements are reflected in all scenarios, and uncertainties are played out differently in the various scenarios.

6 Check scenario themes for consistency and plausibility, considering the time frame and possible outcomes of uncertainties.

7 Develop simple learning scenarios for later debate and development and give them a meaningful name.

8 Identify research needs and collect additional information as needed; re-examine the scenario assumptions.

9 Develop quantitative models if complex interactions need to be assessed.

10 Move toward decision scenarios by re-examining whether the scenarios reflect the real issues faced by the organization and whether they are ready to be shared by others.

FORESIGHT

"Events become indicators of potential change and combinations of events become possible trends. It is about interpreting and pattern matching, making connections, asking 'what if?'"

Foresight is a process by which a fuller understanding of the forces shaping the long-term future is put together. Experts are brought together to develop a vision which is strongly underpinned by a rationale – what are the key factors which are driving us in the direction of this vision? Since Foresight does not claim to predict a certain future situation but recognizes that a range of possibilities exists, it attempts to shape or create paths for development.

The Japanese have the longest uninterrupted use of Foresight, having performed an exercise every five years since 1971. The UK had an exercise involving more than 10,000 people in 1993-5 following on from publication of a Government White Paper, "Realising our potential." This also has a five-year cycle and currently has three thematic and ten sectoral panels. Germany undertook a national Delphi exercise in 1992-3 based on the Japanese approach and later carried out a study on critical technologies. The US approach focuses on critical technologies crucial to improving competitiveness and other societal needs. The US studies have been targeted and of fixed duration, e.g. "the clean car." France and the Netherlands have also favored an approach based on critical technologies. Smaller countries, such as Austria and Sweden, and regions such as Bordeaux in France, have more recently instigated Foresight exercises. Rather than relying on the outputs from any single national program, businesses can access a range of initiatives to survey the differing national expectations.

The process of bringing together a range of experts with influence over the national or local innovation system and stimulating dialog around possible futures is seen as having a positive impact. Georg Aichholzer[5] points out that the function of mobilizing and "wiring up" national innovation systems is itself beneficial. He also sees increasing attention being paid to socio-economic embedding and demand aspects of emerging technologies.

Expectations clearly influence technology strategy. Technological communities share technological visions and the expectations generated lead to the shaping of strategies. In formulating strategies, organizations seek to reduce risk by seeking opinion from experts and stakeholders and building the best-informed foresight they can achieve. But these expectations then shape future actions. One often quoted example is Moore's Law of the doubling of storage capacity on a computer chip in 18-24 months. In the 1980s this became a target for competing chip manufacturers, but it had no scientific basis. It shaped the industry as it underpinned the innovation dynamic. Late delivery had high costs; as chips became more and more expensive to develop, the risks involved increased considerably. Moore's Law became a self-fulfilling "expectancy."[6]

"Foresight may be described both as a production of information, in order to reduce uncertainties about technological development, and as an interaction process between actors to co-ordinate their research, development, and innovation activities. But the resulting information and co-ordination are not like any other. The specific nature of foresight lies in its focus on expectations and its inherent uncertainty because of the unpredictability of the future. The paradox then is that if foresight is successful, organizations reduce uncertainty and improve their ability to develop technology strategies by relying on necessarily uncertain intelligence, rather than on, for example, the certainty of past performance or present markets."

Van der Meulen and Lohnberg (2001)[6]

Certainly Foresight programs are being used by governments to focus research and technology development (RTD) policies and for legitimizing the stance and pose of policy entrepreneurs. In this way expectations about future business prospects are being created. But an important element of the Foresight program is that these visions have also been "tested" for their desirability.

In order to gain the benefits from Foresight, it is necessary to integrate foresight, assessment, and policy evaluation into the business' strategic intelligence system. This strategic intelligence system, whether at the level of the business unit or the business overall, has a major focus on learning and relates closely to the notion of the learning organization. The outcome which the organization is seeking from the exercise is "anticipatory intelligence." Such intelligence is based not only on the "what" but also on the "why" and "how."

COMPETENCE

Probably no other factor has a greater potential impact on future proofing than the firm's current and anticipated future portfolio of core competencies. The idea of core competence, introduced by C.K. Prahalad of the University of Michigan and Gary Hamel of London Business School in 1990,[7] has had a tremendous impact on how firms think about their current and future competitiveness.

At the roots of the core competence perspective is the resource-based view of the organization, a conceptual framework for understanding firm competitiveness using resources as the basic building blocks. In their 1990 *Harvard Business Review* paper, Prahalad and Hamel asserted that core competencies are the outcome of collective learning in the organization. This learning, in turn, is transferred across the organization to enable the creation and embedding of production skills and the bundling of multiple technologies. Firms that successfully identify and cultivate their core competencies can exploit them toward building a position of competitive advantage.

This view has emerged as a counterpoint to market structure analyses of competitive strategy. The resource-based view asserts that it is not the industry structure or the firm's membership in a collective of strategic groups but rather its possession of unique, difficult-to-imitate skills, knowledge, and competencies that endows it with competitive advantage. Other contributions to this perspective have focused on the processes of competence accumulation and management. David Teece, who heads up the Institute of Management, Innovation, and Organization at the University of California, Berkeley, along with his colleagues Gary Pisano and Amy Shuen,[8] has argued that strategically relevant knowledge in the form of capabilities is both tacit (elusive, difficult to transfer and imitate) and subject to learning. Teece and Pisano[9] have extended the notion of competencies to include the dynamic nature of capabilities, arguing that firms' competitive advantage stems from dynamic capabilities rooted in high-performance routines operating inside the organization, embedded in its processes, and conditioned by its history. More recently, the authors, in an earlier work,[10] have developed a methodology for identifying and evaluating the strategic impact of the firm's portfolio of capabilities in terms of competitive impact and competitive strength.

TECHNOLOGY ROADMAPPING

Technology roadmaps are particularly useful at three distinct levels of analysis. National technology roadmaps are used to focus national R&D efforts. At an industry level, roadmapping exercises gather a wide range of expertise to establish a view of the future in terms of possible technology development and timescales. Much of this analysis is in the "pre-competitive domain." Businesses share both national and international information, but each will decide how to utilize this information in its strategy formation and implementation process.

Technology roadmapping within business ventures tends to have a rather different focus. Businesses are seeking more effective responses to the changing competitive landscape – ever more demanding customers, increasingly shorter product life cycles, and fast-changing technologies. In order to improve the product creation process, a long-term view of technology and market developments can improve planning. Many leading-edge technology companies use company-specific roadmaps to pull together those aspects of industry roadmaps which are relevant to themselves. Probably the greatest proponent of technology roadmapping is Motorola, which has practiced it for around 20 years.[11]

Pieter Groenveld,[12] whilst working at Philips Electronics in Eindhoven, the Netherlands, applied the technique extensively and is now a strong advocate of technology roadmapping. He says: "Roadmapping stimulates organizational learning through the encouragement of openness and ways of doing things better. It also supports people at all levels in achieving milestones and becoming committed to their role in the overall process." It would be hoped that roadmaps stimulate creativity and innovation directed with purpose. But the overarching aim of roadmapping is to achieve improved time-to-market and thereby a strengthened competitive position.

It is clear from articles written about roadmapping that many tools exist to support the process, and many organizations develop their own to suit their particular requirements. Other well-understood tools are used in support of the process, such as quality function deployment, maturity grids, and the innovation matrix. But most organizations start the process by defining markets and applications so that products are specified in terms of customer requirements. It is then possible to identify technical functionality for the product and those technologies needed to provide the functionality sought.

Roadmaps may be developed for a product, a range of products, components, or production processes. They may well cross organizational and company boundaries, reflecting the technical complexity of most products. The timescale will vary – the higher the level, probably the greater the timespan. The longer the timescale, the greater the need for visionary thinking, and the more the process will benefit from input from diversity in participants' backgrounds. The various roadmaps developed across the organization need to be reconciled to achieve overall co-ordination of a shared view. Roadmapping is normally an ongoing process. (See Fig. 3.1.)

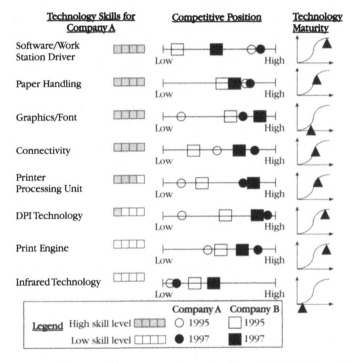

Fig. 3.1 An example of technology roadmapping. (Partovi, F. (1999) ''A quality function deployment approach to strategic capital budgeting,'' *The Engineering Economist*, **44** (3), pp. 239-60.).

The concept of product platforms can be linked to technology roadmapping by identifying the nature and purpose of technologies within systems and on interfaces. When identified, the impact of change in any single technology on other components can be more readily established. The degree of likely disruption can also be predicted and the risks of not gaining some "control" over developments estimated.

QUALITY FUNCTION DEPLOYMENT

Quality function deployment was developed by the Japanese in the 1960s and was first applied in the shipyards at Kobe in 1972. It has since been used in many organizations in the auto, IT, and consumer product industries. Essentially it aims to convert customer demands into quality characteristics to be the basis of a quality plan for the finished product or service. Weighting according to importance of the characteristics and customer desires establishes the overall priorities to be worked towards. The charts also serve to map out what are complex inter-related sets of inputs and outputs.

Figure 3.2 illustrates the application of QFD to an automotive tyre inner tube manufacturer. The chart shows the relationship between customer expectations and design specification. In his article Fariborg Partovi, a specialist in decision sciences from Drexel University, Philadelphia, Pennsylvania, goes further by illustrating how this approach can be extended into project prioritization and capital budgeting decisions.

The Japanese use this approach to identify quality characteristics from customer desires as the first step in the total QFD process. They prioritize the quality characteristics from a customer perspective and use competitive benchmarking to inform the setting of target values. In a second phase the relationship between the quality characteristics and the various design elements is examined, and the component parts of the design are prioritized in terms of desired quality characteristic performance levels. In phase three, the important components are examined in relation to manufacturing processes, with the aim of identifying manufacturing operations that control the component target value, and process target specifications and values are set. Prioritized manufacturing processes and specifications are then used in the final phase to develop work package specifications, control and reaction plans, and training requirements.

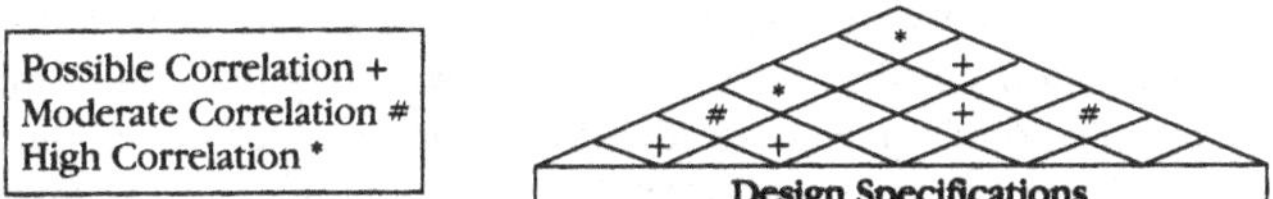

Possible Correlation + Moderate Correlation # High Correlation *								
					Design Specifications			
	1	2	3	4	5	6	7	8
1	Customer Wants	Importance Weights %	Tread Wear Rating	Temperature Rating	Sidewall Rating	Tread Design	Tire Size	Speed Rating
2	Price	24	0.727	0.727	0.727	0.200	0.727	0.200
3	Variety	6	0.200	0.200	0.200	0.727	0.727	0.200
4	Durability	31	0.727	0.727	0.200	0.200		0.073
5	Handling	8	0.073	0.073	0.200	0.727	0.200	0.727
6	Safety	28	0.727	0.200	0.200	0.727	0.073	0.200
7	Environmental Compliance	3	0.200	0.073		0.073		
8	Total	229.3	62.73	47.59	32.05	41.75	25.45	19.68
9	%	100	27	21	14	18	11	9

Fig. 3.2 The relationship between customer expectations and design specification.

Such a comprehensive approach, while seemingly widely adopted in Japan, is not so in the US, where only the first stage is popular with companies such as General Motors and Chrysler.[13] Not only are such techniques used in manufacturing, they are also found in software development, service, and process improvement. They are particularly useful where concurrent engineering is being deployed to cut down time from concept to market.

The technique performs well where good customer data is available – the "voice of the customer." In the US, focus groups and one-to-one interviews are used extensively, whereas in Japan there is more reliance on customer complaints and warranty data. But unless "exciting" customer needs are identified, the product development is unlikely to break the mold. Certainly US companies in the survey by John Cristiano and his colleagues reported a higher level of breakthrough than Japanese companies. The Japanese saw the process as a useful contributor to organizational learning, particularly through using the results in training young engineers.

There is clear merit in combining phase one of the QFD approach – commonly known as the "house of quality" – in a technology roadmapping exercise in order to speculate on customer preferences, needs or demands, and prioritize and then relate these to functionality and to benchmark with competitors. But the approach can also be applied in research portfolio analysis. QFD has been applied in the US National Aeronautics and Space Administration[14] to do just that. The QFD model is used to measure the direct impact of research work packages on the metrics developed for assessing progress towards strategic objectives (SOs). The authors also look at how work packages (WPs) inter-relate to impact on the SOs. They illustrate the approach in relation to one of 10 goals for NASA – "General aviation: Invigorate industry to deliver 10,000 (20,000) aircraft annually (20) years" (see Table 3.1). Table 3.2 shows the SOs and their weighting to meet higher-level goals as well as the associated metrics. Five research work packages are evaluated for their impact against the SOs (see Table 3.3). The interaction between work packages is shown in Table 3.4.

This approach has a number of benefits. In addition to challenging assumptions and raising the level of general awareness of the interactions and importance, it highlights the probability of success and the potential impact of failure on the overall programme. It also allows for adjustment of the SOs over time, possibly de-emphasizing SOs as they approach the achievement of the target metrics and then allowing redeployment of resources to areas where progress is inadequate.

QFD has a place at several points of the future proofing process. First it can support technology roadmapping, which is done as a preliminary to the scenario building. Such an analysis can guide the scenarios because it can give a picture of the technologies likely to impact on customer needs, and how they might do so. The approach is

Table 3.1 Three pillars and ten goals of NASA research[14].

Three pillars	Ten research goals
Global civil aviation: Provide the technical advances to maintain the nation's position in civil aviation	1 *Safety*: Reduce aircraft accident rate by factor of 5 (10) within 10 (20) years 2 *Environmental*: Reduce emissions of future aircraft by a factor of 3 (5) within 10 (20) years 3 *Environmental*: Reduce noise levels of future aircraft by a factor of 2 (4) from today's levels within 10 (20) years 4 *Affordability*: while maintaining safety, triple the aviation system throughput in all weather conditions within 10 years 5 *Affordability*: Reduce the cost of air travel by 25% (50%) within 10 (20) years
Revolutionary technology leaps: Explore technology to revolutionize air travel and create new markets for US industry	6 *High speed travel*: Reduce travel time to the Far East and Europe by 50% within 20 years at today's subsonic ticket prices 7 *General aviation*: Invigorate industry to deliver 10,000 (20,000) aircraft annually within 10 (20) years 8 *Advanced design tools*: Provide design tools to halve the development cycle for aircraft
Access to space: Develop affordable and reliable access to space	9 *Payload cost*: Reduce the payload cost to low earth orbit from $10,000 per pound to $1000 per pound within 10 years 10 *Payload cost*: Reduce the payload cost to low earth orbit from $1000 per pound to $100 per pound by 2020

Table 3.2 Strategic objectives in relation to high level goals[14].

Strategic objective	Weight	Metric description and measures	Base line	Goal
Safety	30%	Fatal accidents per 100k flight hours	1.75	0.5
Affordability	20%	Cost per passenger mile	1.63	0.65
Reliability	15%	Trips per 100 cancelled due to malfunction	3.0	0.25
Weather	10%	Weather cancellations and redirections per 100 trips	10	0.5
Passenger comfort	15%	Combined cabin vibration and noise factors	92	50
Environment	10%	Emissions per operating hour	500	25

Table 3.3 Work packages and their impact on strategic objectives[14].

Strategic objective	Weight	Research work packages				
		Flight systems	Propulsion systems	Integrated design and manufacture	Icing protection	Training systems
Safety	30%	9	9	1	3	9
Affordability	20%	3	3	9	1	9
Reliability	15%	9	9	1	3	1
Weather	10%	9	9	1	9	3
Passenger comfort	15%	1	3	3	1	1
Environment	10%	9	3	1	3	9

Table 3.4 The interaction between work packages[14].

	Flight systems	Propulsion systems	Integrated design and manufacture	Icing protection	Training systems
Flight systems	1.0	0.23	0.23	0.077	0.69
Propulsion systems	0.23	1.0	0.23	0.077	0
Integrated design and manufacture	0.23	0.23	1.0	0.69	0.077
Icing protection	0.077	0.23	0.69	1.0	0.23
Training systems	0.69	0	0.077	0.23	1.0

really more useful for shorter time horizons than those being applied to scenario building; however, at later stages in the overall future proofing process, these charts can help in determining mid-term development of technology by again supporting the roadmapping process. Also, the approach taken by the Japanese in extending the QFD to include manufacturing processes and develop much more detail can be used to test the feasibility of the organization's planned moves.

Organizational learning

Argyris and Schon[15] set the scene for interest in organizational learning. But it was Peter Senge in *The Fifth Discipline*,[16] who gave the topic a degree of practicality, thereby launching it into the mainstream.

John Denton[17] suggests six driving forces behind the need for organizational learning.

1 The shifting importance of factors of production, where the shift is away from land and capital to labor as the predominant production factor.
2 Knowledge as a source of competitive advantage, and as a key antecedent to learning.
3 The increasingly rapid pace of change in the business environment, and the recognition that many businesses are in a period of "permanent white-water."
4 Dissatisfaction with the existing paradigm, where managers are disillusioned with a management paradigm that has not coped with past changes, let alone future ones.
5 The increasingly competitive nature of the business environment, driven by globalization and technology development.
6 Increasingly demanding customers and the need to understand their requirements and respond to them quickly.

An important point for reflection according to de Geus[18] is that "learning begins with perception. Neither an individual nor a company will even begin to learn without having seen something of interest in the environment ... To accomplish this type of learning, the company must see clearly what is happening in its environment. How else can managers know when significant change is necessary, or how to act effectively to achieve a new sort of harmony?'' It is this external stimulus and input to learning which is vital to future proofing.

This link between what we describe as future proofing and organizational learning was made strongly by de Geus with reference to experiences within Royal Dutch Shell over many years. Scenarios were seen as a powerful means for enabling organizational learning. The individual's mental model or cognitive map of the world dictates the manner in which information is labeled or framed, and as actions are later evaluated against scenarios, it is inevitable that these mental models will be tested.

Within Shell managers developed the scenario planning process to include the participants building and playing with software-based simulations based around representations of real worlds, which had the potential to accelerate learning during the scenario building and testing phase. Groups would construct their computer-based model of the organization and its interactions with its environment. When run, the simulation exercises would highlight weaknesses within the model so that participants could reconstruct their world model and retest it. However, after early attempts which appeared quite successful, the facilitators reverted to magnetic boards to draw representations of their models.

Through questioning and discussion, there can be considerable testing of personal assumptions and team-based learning can take place. By using a diverse range of contributors, the implications of scenarios and action plans can be future proofed.

TECHNOLOGICAL DISCONTINUITIES

The notion of technological discontinuities and disruptive technologies is a relatively new idea that has particular relevance in the Internet age. The term ''disruptive technologies'' was coined by Harvard Business School Professor Clayton Christensen and it is the subject of his influential book, *The Innovator's Dilemma*,[19] which appeared in 1997. Disruptive technologies, Christensen explains, are new arrivals on the scene that manage to ''fly under the radar screen'' of the company. These are often companies that diligently go about their business, sustaining their successful product and service offerings. They tend to reject the new arrival because its price is too low and its markets too small. Over time, however, the disruptive technology becomes the next innovation. Often, by that time it is too late to capture the opportunity. Christensen takes the radical position that great companies with rich legacies can fail precisely because they do everything right; that good business practices such as focusing investments and technology on currently profitable products and services can ultimately weaken a successful company. Firms with the best technology tend to work on it, making it even better rather than creating something entirely new. In this way, paradoxically, the very act of "serving the customer well" makes these firms vulnerable.

In his book, Christensen looks at technological changes in various industries. He found a set of recurring patterns emerging that challenged previous innovation theory. Christensen found evidence suggesting that successful practices eventually lead to failure to innovate. He went on to suggest that organizations that want to remain innovative must create and nurture a counter-culture for disruptive technologies within the firm. This counter-culture must be distinctly different from the firm's "sustaining technologies." Key to capturing the opportunity of disruptive technologies is to nurture the right organizational culture and structures that ensure that these new arrivals are properly resourced at the disruptive technology stage.

GAP ANALYSIS

To a large extent, future proofing has to do with closing the gap successfully. Gaps indicate opportunities for firms to improve capabilities for competing more effectively in the future. Gap analysis is largely really about setting the stage for managing change. Change may be triggered by numerous external influences, such as ever decreasing technology cycles, shifting demographics, and globalization, but change ultimately begins in the mind. It starts with new ways of thinking about the future that are later translated into and shaped by new ways of behaving. In thinking about the future, managers must also think about new factors affecting competition that are rewriting the rules of the game.

Organizational knowledge is one such factor. Increasingly, firms are recognizing knowledge as their most valuable and strategic resource. They are beginning to understand that every strategic position is linked to some set of knowledge-embedded resources and capabilities, and that they must deliberately manage these resources in order to remain competitive. The fact that strategically relevant knowledge for the most part exists in the form of the tacit or implicit type presents a particular challenge in itself.

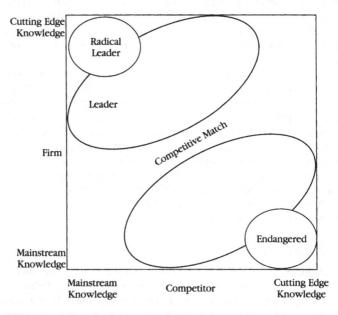

Fig. 3.3 Mapping of a firm's relative competitive position on the basis of access to and control of strategic knowledge. (Adapted from Zack, M. (1999) "Developing a knowledge strategy," *California Management Review*, **41** (3), p. 125.)

The importance of knowledge to the company's competitive position is dependent on its access to, and control of, strategic knowledge relative to its competitor(s). (See Fig. 3.3.) Consequently, there is an inextricable coupling between what the firm believes it *must do* (strategic intent) and the things it *must know*.[20] Both represent future states of the organization. On the other hand, what the firm actually *does know* and *knows how to do* reflects its current capabilities and determines its current competitive limitation(s). The firm's knowledge gap is the difference between what the firm *must know* and what in fact it *does know*.

As suggested in Fig. 3.4, the firm at any point in time has a strategic gap as well as a knowledge gap. These represent the difference between the collective aspirations of the firm with respect to what it *must do* and *must know*, articulated by its value proposition, and its current reality, reflected by what it currently *can do* and *does know*. Inevitably, gaps provide the compelling logic for organizational change; gaps represent opportunities for improvement. Change options can be derived from the outcomes of analyzing the two gaps.

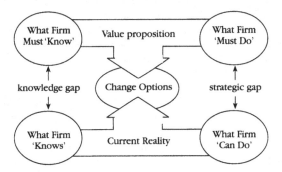

Fig. 3.4 Strategic gaps and knowledge gaps – options for organizational change.

TRENDS ANALYSIS

Future proofing requires that managers understand and interpret socio-economic, technological, and market trends correctly. The origins of trends analysis can be traced to the 1950s when long-range planning was developed for anticipating growth and managing complexity.[21] The assumption was that past trends would continue into the future. Today, keeping up to date with a rapidly changing competitive environment demands sophisticated business intelligence gathering that may include both formal and informal capabilities.

» *Formal capabilities* include virtual and hardwired networks around the world to monitor various developments such as patent applications, scientific and technical developments, processes for searching, filtering and sorting information contained in volumes of published information, and other codified information sources such as the Internet, and a formal system for touching networking with other innovative companies around the world. Formal capabilities may also include formalized techniques such as trend extrapolation, curve matching, Delphi, and relevance trees, scenarios, and cross impact analysis.[22]

Increasingly, the firm is being seen as a boundaryless entity that is tied into networks of firms and communities of commerce; the old "standalone" version of the firm is rapidly disappearing. New game rules and codes of conduct are emerging. The networked firm of the future must learn to position and balance the interests of the network with its own strategic interests and goals.[23]

» *Informal capabilities* draw on informal, largely tacit flows of knowledge between organizations. People are at the heart of these networks; technology merely supports the exchange of information.

There are many approaches to business intelligence gathering. A critical factor is that methods are chosen that consistently bring a diverse array of data that can be used to inform and develop existing business models. Some of these data will fit the models, other data will inevitably not fit. This, however, is desirable since it will force an ongoing re-evaluation and rethink of the current business models, leading to a redoubling of efforts directed at building and nurturing a valid value proposition.

Formal business intelligence involves a variety of analyses that focus on what is happening in the firm's external environment. This external analysis includes the following categories:[24]

» customer analysis – segments, motivations, latent needs;
» competitive analysis – identity, strategic groups, performance, objectives, strategies, culture, cost structure, strengths, weaknesses, new business models;

» market analysis – size, projected growth, profitability, entry barriers, cost structure, distribution system, trends, key success factors, measures of success;
» environmental analysis – technological, governmental, economic, cultural, demographic, scenarios, information needs.

NOTES

1 Schoemaker, P. (1993) "Multiple scenario development: its conceptual and behavioural," *Strategic Management Journal*, **14** (3), pp. 193–214.

2 Wack, P. (1985) (a) "Scenarios: uncharted waters ahead," *Harvard Business Review*, Sept-Oct; (b) "Scenarios: shooting the rapids," *Harvard Business Review*, Nov-Dec.

3 Kloss, L. (1999) "The suitability and application of scenario planning for national professional associations," *Nonprofit Management and Leadership*, **10** (1), pp. 71–83.

4 Schoemaker, P. (1995) "Scenario planning: a tool for strategic thinking," *Sloan Management Review*, **36** (2), pp. 25–30.

5 Aichholzer, G. (2001) "The Austrian Foresight Program: organization and expert profile," *International Journal of Technology Management*, **21** (7/8), pp. 739–55.

6 Van der Meulen, B. & Lohnberg, A. (2001) "The use of Foresight: institutional constraints and conditions," *International Journal of Technology Management*, **21** (7/8), pp. 680–93.

7 Prahalad, C. & Hamel, G. (1990) "The core competence of the corporation," *Harvard Business Review*, **68** (3), p. 79.

8 Teece, D.J., Pisano, G. & Shuen, A. (1990) "Firm capabilities, resources, and the concept of strategy," CCC Working Paper No. 90–8, University of California at Berkeley.

9 Teece, D.J. & Pisano, G. (1998) "The dynamic capabilities of firms: an introduction," in *Technology, Organization, and Competitiveness* (eds Dosi, G., Teece, D.J. & Chytry, J.), Oxford University Press, Oxford, UK.

10 Birchall, D.W. & Tovstiga, G. (2001) "The strategic potential of a firm's knowledge portfolio," in *Crafting and Executing Strategy, Text and Readings*, 12th edn (eds Thompson, A.A. & Strickland, A.J.), McGraw-Hill, Irwin. See also Birchall, D.W. &

Tovstiga, G. (2001) "The strategic potential of a firm's knowledge portfolio," in *Financial Times Handbook of Management*, 2nd edn, (eds Crainer S. & Dearlove, D.), Financial Times Prentice Hall, London.

11 Wheelwright, S. & Clark, K. (1992) *Revolutionizing Product Development*, Free Press, New York.

12 Groenveld, P. (1997) "Roadmapping integrates business and technology," *Research Technology Management*, September-October.

13 Cristiano, J., Liker, J. & White, C. (2000) "Customer-driven product development through quality function deployment in the US and Japan," *Journal of Product Innovation Management*, **17** (4), pp. 286-308.

14 Kauffman, P., Ricks, W. & Shockcor, J. (1999) "Research portfolio analysis using extensions of quality function deployment," *Engineering Management Journal*, **11** (2), pp. 3-9.

15 Argyris, C. & Schon, D. (1978) *Organizational Learning*, Addison-Wesley, Reading, MA.

16 Senge, P., (1990) *The Fifth Discipline – the Art and Practice of the Learning Organization*, Doubleday/Currency, London.

17 Denton, J. (1998) *Organizational Learning and Effectiveness*, p23, Routledge, London.

18 de Geus, A. (1997) *The Living Company*, Nicholas Brealey Publishing, London.

19 Christensen, C.M. (1997) *The Innovator's Dilemma*, Harvard Business School Press, Boston.

20 Zack, M. (1999) "Developing a knowledge strategy," *California Management Review*, **41** (3), p. 125.

21 Aaker, D.A. (1992) *Strategic Market Management*, 3rd edn, John Wiley & Sons, Inc., New York.

22 Goodman, R.A. & Lawless, M.W. (1994) *Technology and Strategy*, Oxford University Press, New York.

23 Tovstiga, G. & Fantner, E.J. (2000) "Implications of the new networked economy for e-business start-ups: the case of Philips' access point," *Internet Research*, **10**, (5).

24 Aaker, D.A. Strategic Market Management, Third Edition, John Wiley & Sons, Inc.

03.10.04

The E-Dimension: Future Proofing

This chapter looks at the impact of recent technological developments and emerging new ways of doing business in an increasingly networked future business environment.

In order to future proof, managers need to develop a better under-standing of the sweeping changes brought on by the Internet. The impact has been profound in the few years since its emergence, leaving virtually no segment of business and society at large untouched. Yet we have probably seen only an inkling of what is still to come.

The great irony of our times, suggests Kevin Kelly,[1] author of *New Rules for the New Economy–10 Radical Strategies for a Connected World*, is that the era of computers is over. Standalone computers have had their day, speeding up our lives a bit perhaps, but not much more. The new future really belongs to technologies that are enabling communication between computers – that is to say, that the future is really about connections rather than computations. Furthermore, since communication is the basis of culture, the new developments are expected to have a momentous impact on every aspect of our lives. Welcome to the age of connectivity and the new networked economy.

The emerging networked economy represents a major upheaval that undoubtedly has had, and will continue to have, an unprecedented impact on how we live our lives and on how businesses will compete in the future. It has three distinguishing characteristics.

1 It is global.
2 It favours intangibles – ideas, information, and relationships; and
3 It is intensely interlinked.[2]

At the root of the new economy lies the Internet and its potential to connect people across organizations, cultures, and business communi-ties. With its emergence, the Internet is driving the creation of a totally new business environment. It has its own distinct opportunities and its own rules. Competition in the new economy demands new orga-nizational forms and entirely new capability sets of firms – capabilities that enable firms to work together in network constellations that bring together customers, suppliers, and even competitors.

The power and value of the Internet and supporting information technologies lies in their capacity to store, analyze, and communicate information instantly, anywhere, at negligible cost. Brad DeLong,[3] an economist at the University of California at Berkeley, suggests that:

". . . IT and the Internet amplify brain power in the same way
that the technologies of the industrial revolution amplified muscle
power."

As technologies are becoming more complex, and competition on a
global scale is intensifying, networks of enterprises are becoming key
to successful innovation. Entirely new business models are emerging
around these networks. These seek to integrate the enterprise in a
virtual Web of customers, suppliers, and other stakeholders, including
distributors and business solution providers. Virtually no industry is
exempt. Not only is the nature of competition changing rapidly, the
very structure of competition is being transformed. Traditionally, enterprises have defined their competition within given industry boundaries.
With the emergence of network-based commerce, boundaries between
markets are blurring. Common to all players is that they use networks
such as the Internet and other electronic media for collaboration and
competition. Traditional rules of competition are being transformed
as enterprises are learning to co-evolve with a diverse and hitherto
unimaginable array of business partners to create value for entirely new
clusters of stakeholders.

The new networked economy has a number of important implications for the firm of the future. All relate to the notion of connectivity.
Kelly suggests that the new rules governing the way in which firms will
think and act in the future revolve around the following axes.[4]

» First, wealth in the future will flow directly from innovation, not
  optimization – it will not be achieved by perfecting the known, but
  rather by imperfectly seizing the unknown. The pace of change will
  not allow companies the luxury of optimizing known routines and
  procedures. The dynamics of the fast-paced networked environments
  will demand that firms within their networks evolve quickly to where
  the opportunities lie. Lou Noto, chairman and CEO of Mobil, took
  his organization through a substantial reorganization to make it more
  fluid and less hierarchical, then likened it to "an irregular electron
  cloud."[5] No doubt more focus and structure would be desirable
  than would be generally provided by electron clouds. The fact of
  the matter is, nonetheless, that traditional approaches to organizing

will not yield the flexibility, adaptability, and, most importantly, the mindset required for continuous and rapid innovation.

» Second, the ideal strategy for cultivating the unknown is to nurture the supreme agility and nimbleness of networks. In the past, managers of established legacy-laden companies concentrated on running their businesses well, building cars perhaps, or selling life insurance policies. There was change, of course, but the world was a relatively orderly and predictable place to do business. Change nowadays has not only become much more rapid, it has also become much more ubiquitous and complex. Connectivity, speed, and the movement of intangibles[6] are blurring the rules and redefining the traditional boundaries of business. We are also seeing product and service offerings merging. Buyers are selling and sellers are buying. We used to have neatly differentiated value chains; now we are facing increasingly messy economic Webs. Finally, there is no longer a clear delineation between structure and process, owning and using, knowing and learning, real and virtual.

» Third, the adoption of the unknown inevitably means abandoning the highly successful known – undoing the perfected. What is it about the Internet that is throwing managers into a dilemma? After all, the Internet is being used in many firms to perform numerous functions that are familiar from the past, albeit much more cheaply and flexibly. E-mail is not so very different from the memo; even the functions that intranets are performing in many ways resemble the enterprise resource planning systems companies implemented and used in the 1990s. New technologies, though, it has been pointed out, often set out mimicking what has gone before – and change the world later. The full potential of the Internet has yet to be realized – just as it took time for companies at the turn of the last century to realize that with electricity they did not need to cluster their machinery around the power source, as in the days of steam.[7] The Internet's chameleon qualities are throwing an additional element of complexity and the unknown into the equation. It is not simply a new distribution channel or a new means of communicating. It is many other things as well, ranging from marketplace to tools for manufacturing of goods and services. Each of these is having an impact on how companies are perceiving their future sphere of business opportunity.

» Lastly, in the ever thickening Web of the networked economy, the cycle of "find, nurture, destroy" happens faster than ever before. New technologies tend to follow an s-shaped trajectory from birth to obsolescence. The beginnings are characterized by a relative shallow slope signifying that they are slow to get started. Once a critical mass is reached, the technology spreads rapidly. The s-curve describes a typical life cycle of a technology that includes the initial phase of discovery and invention, followed by a period along the trajectory in which the technology is developed and market share is captured. Finally, there is a gradual flattening of the curve, signifying a maturing of the technology and the onset of obsolescence. Given the accelerating technology-driven growth and change in every industry, the future will be driven by ever shortening and competing multiple cycles. The maxim of the future will be not to dwell on solving problems but to seek opportunities.

Given these imperatives of the new economy, we will devote the remaining part of this section to a discussion of the networked organization of the future, its drivers and new "distinctive logic," and implications for future proofing.

We will review some of the notions of the new e-economy and the implications for the firm of the future. Major themes include the redefinition of value, the growing importance of knowledge, the new economics of information rather than things, and the emergence of new players such as the infomediary.

» *A new definition of "value."* As industry boundaries blur and wealth creation, communications, commerce, and distribution converge on common networked electronic platforms, providers are being forced to rethink and redefine the notion of value and its creation. Multiple stakeholders in the network clusters demand multiple definitions of value. Traditional, one-dimensional value-chain approaches are no longer adequate. Automobile manufacturers, for example, are reinventing the value offering, providing customers with a service-enhanced electronics package that also ensures mobility.

This is also opening new markets for the automobile manufacturers that previously were claimed by entirely different industry segments. An example would be a "personal mobility package" for motorists that would include not only the automobile and its financing over the service lifetime of the package but also various operational "convenience" aspects, such as onboard navigational devices and their connections to various IT applications, insurance coverage of various types, as well as a service and maintenance package. Consumers would be tied into a value network consisting of a variety of players, but they would interact only in a "one face – one voice" interface to the network. Entire industries are reinventing themselves around new value propositions and business models.

» *The new economics of the networked economy.* The new economy favors intangible things such as ideas, knowledge, and relationships. Information and knowledge form the very bricks of the new networked economy. What is unique about this economy is that a growing portion of production is in the form of intangibles: the exploitation of ideas and knowledge rather than physical things. Wealth creation is occurring in a so-called "weightless economy." Authors Evans and Wurster[8] differentiate between the "economics of information" and the "economics of things." Take, for example, an apple – a thing. If its owner agrees to share it with a friend, both will at best end up with only one half of the apple. When, however, an idea or a tune is shared or sold, the original owner still possesses it and could conceivably share or sell it again. More likely than not, in fact, the idea or the tune would probably improve in value as a result of the exchange. Information and knowledge are said to have "perfectly increasing returns" – they are expensive only to develop; once they are available, they can be reproduced at almost negligible additional cost – for ever.

» *Sharing ideas and knowledge is the maxim of the network economy.* Traditional notions of knowledge is power leading to the hoarding of knowledge (as opposed to land, goods, and resources) is counterproductive and essentially impossible in the new economy. Knowledge and products derived from knowledge are found to obey the law of increasing returns. The sooner and the more widely they are shared and distributed, the greater their value. In commercial terms, the rewards of early entry in knowledge-derived, network-based markets are therefore substantial. Measuring the return on knowledge rigorously, on the other hand, is very difficult, if not impossible as yet. Current accounting methods that date back to the Middle Ages are no longer adequate to capture the real value of knowledge. New metrics are required.

» *Technological innovation as accelerator of growth and change.* Rapid advances in technology – increasingly sophisticated computer software accompanied by leaps in chip development and band-width – are at the root of the unprecedented pace of business all over the globe. New technologies are enabling new forms of orga-nizational learning such as e-learning. After a relatively slow start in the 1980s, e-learning is turning into a multi-billion-dollar industry. Players at the forefront of technological innovation have a significant stake in the new economy.

» *Emergence of the infomediary.* These are intermediaries who sell information about a market and create a platform on which buyers and sellers can carry out business transactions. They can exploit the network's most salient features.[9] For one, this involves the inherent shift of power from provider to client brought on by a reduction in the cost of switching suppliers (the next vendor is only a mouse-click away). Another feature of the network has to do with the substantial reductions in interaction[10] costs that are made possible by digital (Internet) as opposed to physical (telephone) networks. Infomediaries linking buyers and sellers via the Internet can realize substantial savings and efficiencies for both.

» *Disaggregation and specialization.* The speed, range, and accessi-bility of information and the low cost of distribution via the Internet have put infomediaries in a unique position to create new wealth. The knowledge-based value component of a product/service offering, for example, can be enhanced, reconfigured, and customized at each step of the product life cycle to match the value proposition of diverse customers. It can then be redistributed at a premium price. Customers gain both tangible (cost) and intangible (quality) benefits. In this specialist role, infomediaries can often do a better value-adding job than traditional, vertically integrated firms by providing the option of a separate, negotiated product/service offering at each step of the value cycle.

Customers in tomorrow's markets will demand customized products, faster delivery, and instantaneous access to their order status. They will also base their purchase decision on the availability of a wide array of service options. Internet, Web-enabled, and wireless technologies will provide customers with an increasing number of options in an instant of a click. Access to more suppliers and products, pricing transparency – all possible through the Internet – will empower customers to demand highest quality products and services at minimum cost with extended service offerings.[11] In order to deliver on customers' enhanced value demand, the firm of the future will need to develop capabilities for integrating Web-based intelligence into products, manufacturing, and service systems. The technological basis for achieving this extended and enhanced customer value offering will be derived from multimedia-type information-based tools and communications systems that will enable distributed procedures in concurrent engineering design, remote operation of various engineering and business processes, and operation of distributed business systems. Table 4.1, based on the work of Jay Lee,[12] summarizes the implications of e-based business innovation for the firm of the future.

Table 4.1   The implications of e-based business innovation for the firm of the future. (Based on the work of Jay Lee.)

Today's firm	Firm of the future
Focus on data transaction based on e-business:	Focus on performance transaction based on e-business intelligence:
» Respond to customers' needs	» Predict, pre-empt customers' needs
» Enhance customer value	» Optimize customer value
» Achieve customer satisfaction	» Achieve customer intimacy

CASE STUDY: BUCKMAN LABORATORIES
Running a connected business in a networked, global economy

"This [KM] system is dedicated to the front line; it is dedicated to addressing opportunities with customers."
Bob Buckman, president, chairman, and CEO of Bulab Holdings, Inc.[13]

Buckman Laboratories is a Memphis-based speciality chemicals manufacturer that has been a pioneer in creating and living (what does it mean by "and living") knowledge management solutions under the highly visible and visionary leadership of its CEO Bob Buckman. Bob's driving passion has been to empower employees – or associates as they are known – with knowledge through the use of knowledge networking-enhancing technology in order to provide more innovative solutions to the company's customers. Increasing the frequency and the quality of customer contact has been a main driver behind Buckman's networking efforts. For Bob Buckman, the moment of enlightenment came in the late 1980s when he was at home convalescing from a back injury. Two weeks in bed had made him utterly frustrated with his inability to know what was going on at the company. Bob began to map out the vision of a knowledge-driven company connected across all its operations in 80 countries by an electronic network that would allow all its 1200 associates access to the best knowledge-based practices, experiences, and skills. Bob made this vision come true on his return to the office. The results have by far surpassed his original expectations.

Buckman's first initiative to implement structured and systematic capturing and sharing of knowledge came with the introduction in 1988 of the case history system. This was an electronic reservoir of best practices that was to help customers resolve problems faster and more efficiently. Associates in the field were provided access to "Buckman knowledge" about what works well. By mid-1997, Buckman associates could access close to 2500 customer case histories.[14]

Nowadays, the heart of its knowledge network is Buckman's knowledge management and transfer of best practices system called K'Netix®, which was introduced in 1992. Since then, new product-related revenues are reported to have increased by 10% and sales of new products are 50% higher. Response time to customers has been reduced to hours rather than days or even weeks.

The system relies on the participation of Buckman associates around the world. Anyone can post a question on the network and expect to receive a response within 48 hours. An important factor in making the concept work has been Bob's personal drive and visionary leadership role in making Buckman a truly connected enterprise. Every associate has a laptop. This is important given the geographic dispersion of the associates around the globe. More than that, though, everyone is encouraged to let their families play with their laptop and to use the Internet for personal use as well as for business. Thereby, Buckman Laboratories has instilled a cultural norm with a pay-off much beyond the cost to the company – by promoting work at any time and any place. One user has expressed the outcome in the following way: "When you ask one person a question, you have the power of 1200 employees behind you – including our CEO, Bob Buckman."[15]

NOTES

1 Kelly, K. (1997) "New rules for the new economy," *Wired*, September.

2 Kelly, K. (1998) *New Rules for the New Economy – 10 Radical Strategies for a Connected World*, Viking, Harmondsworth.

3 Woodall, Pam (2000) "Survey of the new economy: untangling e-economics," *The Economist*, September 23.

4 Kelly (1997) op cit.

5 Maira, A.N. & Thomas, R.J. (1998) "Organizing on the edge: meeting the demand for innovation and efficiency," *Prism*, Third Quarter.

6 Davis, S. & Meyer, C. (1998) *Blur –The Speed of Change in the Connected Economy*, Warner Books, Reading, MA.

7 (2000), "A survey of e-management: inside the machine," *The Economist*, November 11.

8 Evans, P. & Wurster, T.S. (2000) *Blown to Bits*, Harvard Business School Press, Boston.

9 (1999), "Survey of business and the Internet: the rise of the infomediary," *The Economist*, June 26.

10 Note that we are purposely referring to *interaction* rather than *transaction costs*; the former, we feel, more appropriately describes what happens in a network business process.

11 Lee, J. (2001) "Smart products and service systems for e-business transformation," Key Note Address, PICMET '01, Portland, Oregon, USA, July 29–August 2.

12 Lee, J. (2001) op cit.

13 O'Dell, C. & Grayson, C.J. (1998) *If Only We Knew What We Know*, Free Press, New York.

14 O'Dell, C. & Grayson, C.J. (1998) op cit.

15 Buckman, R. (2001) Presentation, Henley Knowledge Management Forum Workshop, Henley Management College, Oxfordshire, UK, January 22.

The Global Dimension

The implications of an increasingly globalized economy for future proofing are discussed in this chapter.

There are few days when the financial press is not reporting the demise of a once famous organization caught out by the rapid emergence of a competitor which until recently was unknown. In the not too distant past, in a less dynamic world, it was not terribly difficult to notice the new entrant creeping up. For many businesses main customers were located relatively closely, and they would meet regularly and so were aware of their changing needs and preferences. Often, due to a lack of real competition in markets, the supplier had the balance of power in the supplier-customer relationship.

The world has changed dramatically over what really is a relatively short period. But even in these less turbulent times many businesses ignored what in retrospect appeared obvious telltale signs of new and disruptive technology becoming an increasing threat to their survival. Now, however, we all realize that many factors have converged to make it much less likely that we will recognize what is happening in our marketplace. The interconnected world, which one might well assume makes it much easier to understand what is going on around us, is, in reality, making it more difficult for us to keep abreast and comprehend. Interconnectivity has increased complexity and, in turn, uncertainty.

Forecasting has developed as a science, particularly with increasing access to computer processing power. Some features of our future are predictable with a fair degree of certainty, such as the ageing of the population. But when forecasting business futures, increasingly it is recognized that a complex set of variables is involved. These are interconnected in ways which are difficult to map, and many of them contain high levels of inherent uncertainty. Increasing globalization is adding to that uncertainty, not just because competition in many areas of business can now come from anywhere in the world, but also because economic downturns in one financial market can quickly impact another, capital flows are largely unrestricted, many global organizations have assets in excess of some nation states and can exert ever more influence over governments, and labor is increasingly unrestricted by location. All these unpredictable aspects of the new world order bring into question the validity of any forecasting of business futures.

There has been much talk about the move to the new economy which is emerging based around the knowledge economy, enabled as it is by the interconnectivity offered through the Internet. Few businesses are escaping the impact of the World Wide Web, whether in terms of communicating with customers and suppliers, seeking out information, purchasing supplies, advertising jobs, advertising and selling services or goods, or transferring work to other locations and organizations. And since the Internet is not controlled by physical boundaries, this activity is going on globally and therefore much of it is not measured by official statistics so the extent is largely unknown. Traditional approaches used to control the deployment of resources within a hierarchical structure no longer work in what has become a fast-moving, competitive landscape.

But more dramatically, what is being seen is the emergence of new business models. There is a serious challenge to many traditional supply chains as reorganization, often driven by global businesses facing growing worldwide competition, has led to restructuring driven by cost economics and enabled by information and computing technology. New suppliers have used the power of information and communications technology (ICT) to attack the most profitable parts of supply chains – notable examples being Charles Schwab and Amazon – thus creating a major challenge to old-world businesses. Traditional hierarchy is under threat as the "machine model" of organization can no longer keep pace with the rate of change demanded. The emerging forms of organization are essentially based on the principles of networked and virtual communities coming together to satisfy specific customer needs and disbanding once those needs can no longer generate the profits being sought. These transient organizations can now be as readily formed from a global mix as from within a local marketplace or a one-nation state.

The features of the new economy are shown in Fig. 5.1. We see knowledge to be at a high premium; information replacing physical assets in importance to the success of organizations; highly competitive global markets for customers, human, and financial resources; customers having much greater power of choice; and if organizations are to remain competitive, the need for innovations which are much more radical than we have seen in the past.

While globalization is possibly seen as a threat by many businesses, it also offers opportunities. Where technology is developing rapidly, organizations can much more readily locate the "hot spots"

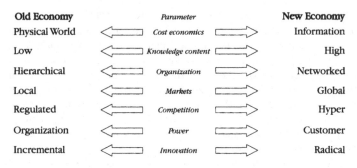

Old Economy	Parameter	New Economy
Physical World	Cost economics	Information
Low	Knowledge content	High
Hierarchical	Organization	Networked
Local	Markets	Global
Regulated	Competition	Hyper
Organization	Power	Customer
Incremental	Innovation	Radical

Fig. 5.1 The implications of the move from the old world to the new knowledge-based economy.

of development – physical or virtual clusters of businesses with high levels of knowledge and expertise – and make contact and form relationships to support their own business objectives. The same applies to entry into new markets, e.g. online information from trade organizations is available to give instant information to even the smallest exporters and investors, partnering can be brokered electronically, and arrangements made to review markets and partnership possibilities. By sharing technology development, risk exposure can be reduced, new combinations of technology can be identified, and new products be generated. Virtual meeting places, unbounded by time and space, give the opportunity to join communities of practice for knowledge sharing, clearly an important source of intelligence about what is happening within the global environment as well as an opportunity to enhance personal knowledge and expertise.

The Internet not only offers opportunities to organizations to remodel themselves and their supply chains and do business in different ways, it also gives the same access to other stakeholders to monitor the behavior of businesses and mobilize responses, whether done on the Internet or by direct protest, such as at recent G7 meetings. Environmental groups can be much better informed about environmental issues through the sharing of scientific evidence via the Web. But they can also monitor the activities of global organizations as people report local activities globally. This can of course be highly damaging to the reputation and image of the firm – something which not only impacts customer attitudes but also can lower the workforce's morale. In building scenarios, environmental risk is an important consideration, but where organizations market and sell goods and services into foreign markets, and source, manufacture, or outsource manufacturing across national boundaries, whether intentionally or not, this has to be put into a global context. Beyond this is the increasing interest among stakeholders in good citizenship on the part of business, which embraces good practice employment as well as the fair treatment of customers and suppliers.

It is now not unusual to find companies of all sizes outsourcing work to countries outside their place of established operations. Some have considerable experience of using services such as call centers outside their home country. But many move design work from center to center across the globe so that operations can take place 24 hours per day. Clear clusters of expertise have emerged (for instance, software development in Bangalore) which now serve the global market for services. So we are detecting not only a concentration of expertise in areas, but also the consolidation of what were already large enterprises – an obvious example is in the pharmaceuticals industry with the formation of GlaxoSmithKline which embraces also Beecham.

Companies are also rapidly reshaping themselves and moving in and out of markets. ABB with its move from manufacture to service provision;[1] GE's failed attempt to acquire HP to enhance its service offering; the takeover of E&Y Consulting by what many believed was an IT services company, Cap Gemini; the transformation of GEC from an engineering company to a telecommunications R&D, manufacturer, and service company, Marconi. Another of our case examples traces the history of Buckman Laboratories[2] as it transformed itself from a manufacturer of chemicals to a provider of services to the pulp and paper industry in more than 80 countries.

So what we see is a rapidly changing business landscape as firms struggle to establish themselves in the most favorable long-term markets in their attempt to capitalize on their unique assets and capabilities. But decisions which appear sound and well founded in today's world can quickly look disastrous in periods of turbulent change. Take Marconi, which moved from a rather staid but very successful engineering company, GEC, put together by Lord Weinstock over a working lifetime, into a business focused on the telecommunications industry. In the short period as the firm was engineered in the late 1990s and early 2000, this looked like an excellent move. The share price more than matched the rise in the industry generally. But in 2001, with the downturn in the industry, Marconi probably suffered more than its rivals due to a number of errors made by executive management, such as a failure to recognize first how rapidly the market was changing, then to take swift compensatory action, and also to keep stakeholders informed. Certainly 12 months was a short time in which to plummet from the giddy heights to the depths. In hindsight, one would of course have advised against the dramatic move to focus solely on telecommunications equipment. It is interesting, however, that ABB, which acquired the power company GEC-Alstom, in which GEC was formerly a joint venture, has also left the industry.

GE, in seeking to take over Honeywell, ran foul of European-level government regulatory authorities in the form of monopolies concerns. A similar fate has befallen British Airways as it has attempted mergers with US airlines and others, and has been blocked by government authorities on both sides of the Atlantic. The banking sector in the UK also ran into government intervention, but this time within the UK, standing in the way of a merger between Lloyds TSB and the Alliance and Leicester, a former building society, on the grounds that it would seriously impact on customer choice. Companies are finding the route to achieving their strategic intentions blocked by governments seeking to protect the interests of the public or in some cases their own domestic industries.

So how is this affected by globalization? As organizations seek to consolidate in order to work with other global players, they are likely to become dominant within sectors of their industries. Governments and international agencies are becoming more concerned about the impact of this trend on their economic prospects, and the threat that it poses.

Government policy can have a major impact on the returns from investments by overseas organizations. The impact of large foreign-owned OEMs (own equipment manufacturers) on the future of a local supplier company is illustrated in one of the cases.[3] The national government in Malaysia has a positive policy toward companies seeking inward investment. It expects any company locating a manufacturing base to develop its local supply base. Many OEMs offer support to local entrepreneurs in the form of financing, training, access to technical support, and long-term contracts. But these companies put high demands on their suppliers to achieve long-term quality improvements and price reductions, and to cope with fluctuating demand patterns. The local companies are also vulnerable to local wage inflation and currency fluctuations as their countries become more prosperous – factors which make transfer to lower-wage economies attractive for the OEM.

TWO SCENARIOS CONSTRUCTED BY SHELL (FROM /WWW.SHELL.COM)

1. *TINA* (There is no alternative)
Above – Globalization, liberalization, technology – and their interactions

Globalization, liberalization, and technology innovation improve efficiency and enable new products but also create effects whose impacts take years to understand, e.g. IT informs customer choice and influences buying patterns; IT disintermediates, giving customers direct access to manufacturers; IT enables communications, automation, tracking, and speed.

Implications: The squeeze on societies and institutions will intensify. Global rules will be designed for the evolving business game to enable fair play and efficiency and a strengthening of global institutions.

2. *TINA* Below – People with education, wealth, and choice

People are increasing in wealth and education and have more choices. They exercise choice based on values and desires rather than necessity. They are more willing to pay for goods and services that are environmentally friendly from companies that exercise social responsibility.

> **Implications**: People power creates new kinds of economic activity and challenges business to be more creative and resilient.

In an interconnected world where there are intricate inter-relationships between the factors on which business success is dependent and no way of precisely modeling behaviors, traditional methods of strategic planning, based on sophisticated forecasts, are no longer possible. The world is just too complex for any company, no matter how great its resources, to produce a plan based on a scientific approach. Under these circumstances scenarios offer a way forward in mapping out a future.

On its Website[4] Shell identifies some of the questions which, in the view of its planners, the global organization has to address and which can be applied to and addressed in various scenarios.

» What does it mean to be a global company?
» What strategic control points can enable businesses to gain sustainable advantage?
» Does unbundling businesses within a corporation improve performance?
» What risks are important, and how can they best be managed?
» Where are the profit zones – areas where customers are willing to pay more than the cost of capital?
» What do companies need to learn in order to perform better? How can they learn more effectively?
» How much authority should be delegated to front-line managers, and what processes and organizations are needed for such empowerment?
» Technology has enabled companies to organize in networks. Are such organizations advantageous, and if so, where and how?
» Where should businesses provide tailored solutions for different situations and different customers, and where should they offer an optimized single solution?
» How can a high-level value proposition be translated into practical business strategies?
» What is the best approach to technology development and commercialization?

TWO GLOBAL SCENARIOS BASED ON THE WORK OF PETER SCHWARTZ[5]

Descent into anarchy

Drivers:

» Little growth in employment.
» Income gaps widening.
» Crime and terrorism on the increase.
» Environmental decay mounting.
» Weak political leadership in the OECD.
» Increase in trade disputes.
» Volatility in currencies.
» Ethnic cleansing in a number of countries and regions.
» Anti-immigrant fever.
» Politics of identity.

The scenario

Conflict between the US and Russia due to upheavals in central Asia, drug lords control much of the developed world, ethnic conflicts on the increase as well as terrorism in the US. This is despite a growing global economy, but with "haves" and "have nots." Pessimism results from less stability rather than a lack of prosperity, which is due to economic struggle and change; accelerating technological change; widening income gap; growth in Asia but collapse in Russia and Africa; end of cold war constraints on conflict.

Surfing the net waves

Drivers:

» Productivity growth in the US.
» New technology is pervasive.
» Growth potential increasing.
» Multilateral co-operation developing.
» Global trade barriers reducing.

» Asia on the move and South America growing economically.
» Central Europe improving.
» Responding to environmental issues.

The scenario

Technology reach is creating opportunities everywhere, but a number of challenges have to be met, including joint peace-keeping efforts in Central Asia and the Middle East; improved education everywhere; structural changes to make technology more accessible; low tolerance for violence and effective action; World Trade Organization effectiveness; tackling the sources of crime; inclusion of China and India in the first order of nations; new environmental conflict resolution methods.

The ABB, Buckman Laboratories, and LIH case studies illustrate how companies can use scenarios to develop a route forward, to identify resource needs, and to guide action.

To help businesses look at the global implications, scenario building needs to:

» take a holistic view in constructing scenarios to include a global perspective and multivariable analysis;
» call on appropriate experts and thought leaders, wherever located, to assist in the process and also to respect their inputs;
» use highly diverse teams to work on the scenarios and future proofing to reflect global perspectives and experiences;
» ensure that language or cultural differences do not inhibit experts' contributions;
» accelerate learning across the organization and across organizational boundaries to embrace a global view into organizational learning; develop a seeking culture and one where insights about the impact of globalization get passed on and discussed within the organization;
» systematically record and analyze comments on the global aspects of the scenarios;
» test the scenarios at regular intervals and with as broad a group as possible;

» adopt a mentality in which flexibility in planning is given high value;
» seek out and share with global organizations best practice processes for scenario building.

NOTES

1 See the case study in Chapter 7.
2 See the case study in Chapter 7.
3 See the case study in Chapter 7.
4 Shell Website http://www.shell.com
5 Ringland, G. (1997) *Scenario Planning - Managing for the Future*, pp. 146-7, Wiley, Chichester.

The State of the Art

This chapter presents and discusses the key issues relating to future proofing and looks at the current debate on the subject.

KEY ISSUES AND CURRENT DEBATE

Prior to the nineteenth century explorers would set out on grand expeditions into the unknown without a map. Many would not even be able to see very far ahead as they hacked their way through heavy undergrowth. At best they had a compass to guide them, a timepiece, and the rising and setting of the sun and the position of the stars. Before the development of the chronometer by John Harrison,[1] a UK cabinet maker, in the eighteenth century, navigation methods were so suspect that ships would land miles away from their intended destination. But any sensible explorer kept a meticulous log of the journey so as to have a reasonable chance of being able to return to the starting point.

One might look at the direction of organizations as a journey into the unknown. Often people think they know from whence they have come, but even this is likely to be hazy as they won't have kept a detailed log and in any case each person will have mentally recorded the journey differently. But being able to recall the journey is of little value in an organizational setting today. Putting back the clock is not an option, nor is adopting the assumptions underlining the "old model."

But just like the old-time explorer, organizations can put together a clear vision and win the commitment of stakeholder groups to that vision. They can set themselves stretch targets as a focus for collective achievement. In moving along this unknown journey, clearly the wise navigator seeks the best tools available to help plot a route. Organizations have a distinct advantage over the old-time explorer in that they have access to resources which go well beyond the equivalent of the explorer's "crew" and which have much more experience of charting the unknown. And these resources are becoming more and more accessible in real time as information and communications technology improves.

In this section we will look at how the organization of the future will find better ways of future proofing; how technology will aid the process; but also at the need for a different form of leadership, better able to cope with the uncertainties facing organizations of any size as the implications of globalization reach broader and deeper. We will look at how organizations can build a portfolio designed along the principles of future proofing.

EMERGENT IDEAS AND CONCEPTS

Inevitably, closing the gap between the firm of today and the envisioned firm of the future requires organizational change of some sort or another. Indeed, change has become the one constant of modern management, perhaps its most important imperative. Learning to adapt, being able to respond to change, and turning external change into competitive advantage have perhaps become the top priorities of management today. In order to narrow this difference, firms must embark on a path of change.

But how do managers go about closing the gap? The gap is defined by two points along the time horizon of an organization. One might also think about the time line in terms of the business focus. In the present, the focus will be operational and tactical; the firm will be concerned with maintaining a strong competitive position "today for today." Looking into the future, the business focus will be strategic; the firm will focus on "today for tomorrow." Thus, the gap represents the difference between the current point representing today's firm and a point in the future that describes the envisioned firm of the future in terms of a number of likely scenarios (Fig. 6.1). The gap might be thought to represent a number of differences between the two states of the firm – it may be the difference in the two firms' portfolios of capabilities, or between their ways of thinking, their paradigms. It may also be the difference in their cultures and organizational mindsets.

The gap may represent time frames which span years, hence managers require mental models and approaches to help them think about the future and the path to get there. We can imagine two approaches for thinking about the future.

Looking forward from the present

Applying this approach, we start by examining the present situation, the here and now. From the analysis of the present, important short-term issues are identified. Measures to resolve these issues are defined and brought to action. Short-term, tactical issues are thus the primary drivers for change. A particular danger lurking when this approach is taken is that the urgent may displace the important. This approach has the advantage that short-term problems are resolved. The cost, however, may be that the firm fails to focus on the broader, long-term

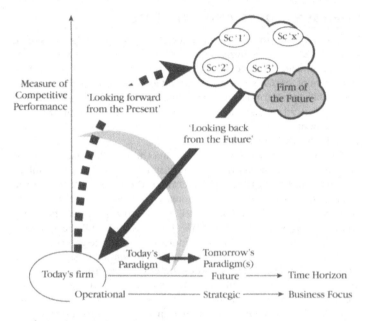

Fig. 6.1 Bridging the gap between the firm of today and the firm of tomorrow – two approaches: looking forward from the present and looking back from the future.

issues and challenges that may be key to building a strong competitive position in the future.[2]

Looking back from the future

In applying this approach, the concerns of today's firm are still important, but they are balanced with a compelling vision of the future. This vision brings in the thinking of many people of the organization; it concerns the needs of the firm of the future in terms of organizational structures, culture and values, skills and capabilities, process and knowledge. This approach has the power to make many people in the organization think about the future in such a way that it is possible to begin to think about possible pathways of change that will lead to the future, pathways that succeed in bridging the realities of today and the envisioned future of tomorrow's firm.

On the basis of the second approach, we will now introduce and develop a number of ideas, management concepts, and techniques for future proofing (Fig. 6.2).

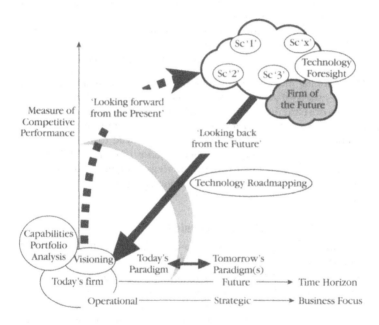

Fig. 6.2 Concepts and techniques for future proofing.

Visioning

Visioning involves the capability and capacity to create and develop a vision of the future that is compelling, bold, and engaging. It must excite and capture the imagination of all stakeholders as much as it must provide a shared view of what could be possible and how it might be achieved.[3] Visioning can take several forms. Generally, it addresses the questions: What business *are* we in? What would we *like to be* in, in the future? What type of an organization are we? What type would we like to be? What is our strategic vision? Is it widely shared throughout the organization?

Answers[4] to these questions would include a specification of the:

» business scope – markets the firm chooses to compete in, and those it chooses not to compete in;
» intentions with respect to future growth – potential markets and technologies of the future; and
» key resources, assets, and capabilities on which the firm is based.

The visioning process can then be used for generating and screening a wide variety of strategic options. Another outcome of the visioning process can be a (re)definition of the business for employees, customers, and other stakeholders that captures the essence of the firm's purpose, identity, and commitment. This exercise can lead to useful insights, particularly if the business is defined in terms of current (and future) customer needs rather than product offerings. In doing so, Xerox Corporation, for example, moved from defining its business as "copiers" to the "document" company.

Capabilities portfolio analysis

The capabilities portfolio analysis is a management methodology developed by Birchall and Tovstiga[5] for assessing the strategic impact of a firm's portfolio of capabilities. The methodology is based on a number of underlying premises. First, a firm's knowledge manifests itself in the firm's capabilities. Second, organizations cannot manage what they don't know they have. The methodology is a knowledge mapping tool in this sense. It helps managers to identify their current capabilities, thereby providing a measure of the firm of today in terms of what it knows and its capabilities in terms of their competitive impact and strength. The methodology does more than this, however, it helps guide managers' thinking about what capabilities the organization will require in the future. The methodology highlights the firm's "white spaces" – opportunities that the firm can exploit. Thereby the methodology is also a strategic analysis tool.

The methodology begins with a mapping of any one of the firm's business processes from a value-creation perspective. Implicit here is the assumption that knowledge must contribute to the firm's value-generation process. One of the core business processes is then selected and examined in terms of its key success factors. Capabilities that deliver on these factors are then identified and prioritized. A set of important capabilities is subsequently selected and classified according to competitive impact (maturity) and competitive position (firm's position of strength with respect to the particular capability). Degree of tacitness is used as an indicator of the firm's position of strength with respect to a particular capability; the greater the degree of tacitness, the more the capability represents a unique competitive feature of the firm.

Once the firm's portfolio of capabilities has been mapped according to its competitive impact and competitive strength (see Fig. 6.3), the resulting map can be used to show how new knowledge and capabilities can be brought into the firm.

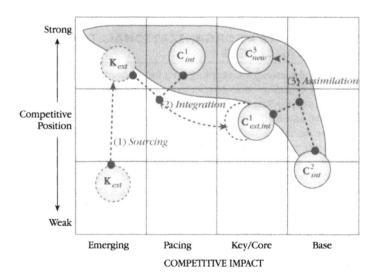

Fig. 6.3   The capabilities portfolio and the knowledge acquisition trajectory.

Capability C_{int}^1 is a strategically important capability for the firm and one over which it has considerable control. It is "emerging" in that it is supporting products and services which are just becoming important in the marketplace and hence leading edge. C_{int}^2, on the other hand, is a capability which is supporting products and services which have become commoditized and therefore is readily replicated by other firms. K_{ext}, in contrast, is a knowledge domain which is emerging and has a strong likelihood of impacting on the products or services offered by the firm in the future. It is an area where mastery is expected to become important for competitive positioning, and therefore greater control is desirable. The potential offered for integration with existing capabilities for assimilation with other capabilities to form recombinations which address new market needs is shown in Fig. 6.3, where C_{new}^3 represents a capability over which the firm has secured a high degree of control which has been built on a strong capability which had over time become weak in terms of market position. An assessment of risks associated with alternative strategies can be made to support executive decision making.

IMPLICATIONS AT ORGANIZATIONAL, TEAM, AND INDIVIDUAL LEVELS

The principal reason for embarking on a future proofing exercise is to prepare the organization more effectively to meet the challenges of the future. Future proofing is a process and not a technique, although tools, techniques, and methodologies can support the process. Its value lies less in the actual scenarios produced or even the plans for action but rather in the process in itself and the way in which it can "galvanize" action. It is not intended as an academic exercise or one which is undertaken exclusively by an executive team or specialist group. To maximize the benefits it needs to embrace the organization and lead to a new way of looking at the future. It needs to heighten curiosity about what is happening in the business environment and to promulgate a culture of sharing, debate, and initiation.

So at an organizational level there is the need for board-level commitment to the process. There is the need for both formal structures and informal meeting points to enable widespread engagement in the process. There is the need for visibility and effective communication.

To be engaged people need to have access to the information on which judgments are being made. Also there is the need to expose, critique, and rebuild mental models. Above all there is the need to secure the commitment of all those stakeholders involved in the process.

Organizational learning is a process which is very much based around teams: project teams, working parties, operational teams, informal teams. A culture of reflection, questioning, sharing, and action taking is essential to the process if it is to be effective. Aligning reward systems with a culture of team working is a prerequisite. An embedded culture of individualism based among others things on individual performance-related rewards is normally not conducive to the future-proofed organization.

For the individual, whether within an organization or not, where flexible response to changing environmental conditions is paramount, there is considerable emphasis being placed on training and development. On the one hand the organization needs to develop specific capabilities underpinned by knowledge and the competence of individuals, but on the other it needs people who have broad-based interests who will bring alternative perspectives to any debate and decision making. So organizations need in-depth expertise in specific areas but also people who are able to take a helicopter view with a holistic/systems view approach.

However, given that many now see the half-life of knowledge being six months at most, the individual cannot afford to have one area only of in-depth knowledge and expertise without having a half-developed competence in some emerging area. Individuals, just like organizations, in planning their future can apply the principles of future proofing by careful research and review and then placing bets on those emerging areas which are of personal interest and developing their competence so that there is sufficient breadth in their knowledge that they can quickly master new areas. This again suggests the application of the concept of a technology platform – the identification of some underlying competences which can be easily applied in new or different fields.

The style of leadership is clearly vital for the future-proofed organization. Success depends largely on "shared" leadership rather than on the central charismatic personality. The process of future proofing depends on contributions and challenge from all parts of the organization and beyond. It depends not only on visionary thinking but also on the capacity to change swiftly to meet emerging opportunities and personal skills in gaining commitment to the process of collective learning – "anticipating opportunities, learning from others, developing and empowering people and living the values."[6]

LIKELY TRENDS AND DEVELOPMENTS IN FUTURE PROOFING

There is little doubt that generally if organizations are to survive they will have to increase the pace at which they renew themselves. If one accepts this assertion it can then be assumed that organizations will show increasing interest in how to future proof. Yet given the rate of change (technological, economic, social, and environmental), and the increased complexity of decision making, the likelihood of effective future proofing will reduce.

Organizations will use ICT to an increasing extent to support future proofing. Knowledge management is one area which is high on the organizational agenda as we move deeper into the knowledge economy. Knowledge management systems can have considerable impact on the organization's capability to future proof by:

» providing information sources to support the process throughout and enhance the quality of decision making;
» offering electronic tools such as group systems to enable the effective distribution of activities such as brainstorming, ideas sharing, and collective evaluation;
» providing access to experts around the world in real time and asynchronously;
» storing the outputs of discussions, model building, and review;
» managing the work flow to put together the scenarios and action plans, and for regular monitoring;
» increasing the reach of the activity and speeding up the process;
» providing tools to improve forecasting capability, risk assessment, portfolio management, and other areas vital to developing future proofing.

As societies become more affluent overall, the issues of concern change. This can be seen in relation to environmental considerations. The added complexity of decision making as new issues emerge in importance adds to the difficulties in future proofing and makes the dependence on high-capacity computing power greater. But given these intellectual challenges, people's inventiveness will also be challenged as they look for new ways of improving the application of techniques such as modeling. So the need for future proofing will increase, the tools will improve, and through experience people's capabilities will develop.

NOTES

1 The story is told in Sobel, D. (1999) *The Illustrated Longitude*, Fourth Estate, London.

2 Gratton, L. (2000) *Living Strategy*, Financial Times Prentice Hall, Harlow.

3 Gratton, L. (2000) op cit.

4 Akers, D. (1992) *Strategic Market Management*, 3rd edn, John Wiley & Sons, Inc., Chichester.

5 Birchall, D.W. & Tovstiga, G. (2001) "The strategic potential of a firm's knowledge portfolio," in *The Financial Times Handbook of Management*, 2nd edn (eds Crainer, S. & Dearlove, D.), Financial Times Prentice Hall, London; see also Birchall, D.W. & Tovstiga, G. (2001) "The strategic potential of a firm's knowledge portfolio," in *Crafting and Executing Strategy – Text and Readings*, (eds Thompson, A.A. & Strickland, A.J.), McGraw-Hill Irwin Publishing, Burr Ridge, IL.

6 Solomons, J., Hu-Chan, M., Mann, C.E. & Robertson, A.G. (2000) "Becoming an effective global leader," in *Coaching for Leadership*, (eds Goldsmith, M., Lyons, L. & Freas, A.), Jossey-Bass, San Francisco.

07

In Practice: How Companies Tackle Planning

This chapter presents a number of case studies showing how organizations are future proofing.

INTRODUCTION

Scenario planning has the power to develop an array of plausible futures from which strategic options can be drawn. It is then possible for executives to plan a way ahead for the organization which is the "best fit" given the scenarios, but one which is based on a reasoned compromise between demands for "lean operations" and for "unlimited flexibility" for maneuver.

We present four cases which offer interesting contrasts. Each case has been selected because it illustrates different features of the future proofing approach. No one case is complete in itself in the sense that it presents a full application of the approach to future proofing that we advocate, partly because in practice executives use concepts and tools to support decision making in a discriminatory way, not letting themselves be governed by prescriptive methodologies. The process of future proofing requires intuition as well as analysis. At the end of the day the executives responsible for determining the business' future have to use tools and techniques such as these in ways which provide the best fit to the problem situation and their style of operation.

The first case is based on a very successful US speciality chemicals company in private ownership. The company was led for many years by the visionary Bob Buckman, who transformed it from a chemicals producer to a full global service provider within the markets in which it specialized. We describe possible scenarios over a 20-year period and look at the implications for capabilities development at each phase.

The second case also describes a transformation. It is the story of ABB, which grew following the merger between the two engineering giants ASEA, a Swedish company, and Brown Boveri, based in Switzerland. Not only did it grow into one of the world's most successful companies, but it is making a major strategic move out of its traditional engineering businesses into service provision. This case identifies the drivers and the transition, as well as the rationale underpinning it. It demonstrates how a company is adopting future proofing principles to redesign itself.

The next case is in quite different circumstances but with equally challenging issues to face up to, albeit of a different type. This Malaysian company has grown rapidly and has been part of the Malaysian economy success story. It produces components which have been in high demand but which are built into products which are extremely sensitive to recession. Much of the company's work is done for major Japanese and other manufacturers which contract manufacture of components into areas where semi-skilled labor is more plentiful and less costly. But its internal customers are also impacted by any downturn in either the local or international markets. The company recognizes these vulnerabilities as it seeks to decide its direction.

The company described in the fourth case study is much younger and in a fast-growing mobile telecommunications market. It is a provider of cellular telecommunications services to consumers and businesses in the United Kingdom. The company's share of the growing market for mobile telecommunications operators (telco) grew dramatically from 7% of the market in 1995 to 24.5% in 2000. When the boom started, the company's executives asked themselves: what next? This case study outlines the scenario planning process that the telco used to plan for continued success while taking into consideration various forces and contingencies that could affect the future of the telecommunications industry.

BUCKMAN LABORATORIES

From chemicals producer to full global service provider

Since being founded in Memphis, Tennessee in 1945 by Dr Stanley Buckman, Buckman Laboratories has been a leading manufacturer of speciality chemicals for aqueous industrial systems. It has more than 20 associate companies worldwide, and operates in more than 80 countries, marketing and selling more than 1000 speciality chemicals manufactured in eight factories.

The company believes it is important to maintain its focus on innovative technology in providing solutions for a customer's paper mill, cooling system, or tannery. Additionally, the annual report indicates that the firm aims to significantly enhance its existing solutions "with unique programs designed for the needs of our customers' employees with whom we collaborate."

In its annual report (2000) the company makes a very strong statement about its purpose and mission:

"Our purpose at Buckman Laboratories is to carry out our Mission – to excel in providing measurable, cost-effective improvements in output and quality for our customers by delivering customer-specific services and products, and the creative application of knowledge.

By fulfilling our Mission, we create customer value and earn an acceptable return for our shareholders. The services and products we deliver are designed around the needs of the customer."

While Buckman Laboratories supplies a range of industries such as paper and pulp, water treatment, coatings and plastics, leather, wood, and agriculture, this case example focuses on pulp and paper.

We have used a historical perspective to illustrate possible uses of scenarios to aid in creating a strategic intent and then to gain some insights into the capabilities essential to make attainment possible. We have presented three scenarios, each one intended to reflect a 10-year horizon.

Possible scenarios for paper and processing – 1980

Scenario 1: Full steam ahead

» Increasing wealth of nations.
» Paper and paper-based products in growing demand.
» High-quality paper – growth particularly strong.
» Packaging materials – increasing as customers increase quality requirements.
» Strong competition among pulp processors but no major new players as capital costs high and returns low.
» Pollution from processing plants of increasing concern within local areas.
» Steady improvement in processing plant efficiency due to improvement in chemical control.

Scenario 2: Rough seas

» The increasing turbulence in world economy.
» Newsprint in decline due to increasing dominance of TV in securing advertising revenue.
» Substitute materials used for packaging.
» Oversupply of paper and pulp products leading to overcapacity and rationalization among manufacturers.
» Chemical suppliers consolidate to ensure protection of markets by acquisition of R&D outputs.
» Price and impact on efficiency dominate purchase decisions.

Scenario 3: Rocks just below the surface

» While the world economy overall is making progress, new processing plant in developing countries threatens established facilities.
» Environmental pressures in developed countries exacerbate the competitive threat of new capacity in developing countries where regulation is minimal.
» Companies based in low-cost economies increasingly win supply contracts for chemicals used in processing.
» Increasing demand for paper and pulp-based products from developing countries does not compensate for lost markets in developed countries.
» Rationalization of manufacturers impacts on suppliers by reducing the number of potential customers. Some suppliers re-orientate their businesses to more lucrative markets, those slow to change either get acquired or cease trading.

Faced with these possible scenarios, these were Buckman's intentions.

» A move from being multinational to global, with decision making taken to the business-customer interface and away from the center.
» To move from being a product-focused to a customer-driven business.
» To improve its 49% capacity utilization by increasing sales capacity and effectiveness.

Table 7.1 Capabilities needs resulting from the 1980s scenarios.

Knowledge and understanding	Technology	Management	Culture
Knowledge of clients' needs, means, and methods High-level problem solving based on scientific knowledge and holistic understanding	R&D to ensure strength in aqueous industrial systems Systems to enable best practice to be shared across the globe	Delegation to local units Empowerment of front-line staff Seen to be "walking the talk" Targetted on innovation and new product development Environmental scanning and competitor analysis	"One company" feel wherever based Relationship building with customers Set of shared values A "sharing" culture where expertise is rewarded when applied to client problem solving

» To develop a multicultural, multilingual organization sharing a common understanding of how we should relate to each other and to outsiders, captured in a new company code of ethics.
» To invest in R&D to ensure world leadership in specialist products.

The capabilities needs resulting from the 1980s scenarios are shown in Table 7.1.

Possible scenarios for paper and pulp processing – 1990

Scenario 1: The "clipped" swan

» Concern about expansion of the world's economy being limited by finite natural resources.
» Global warming leading to stricter controls on environmental impact of processing plants.
» New packaging materials impacting on markets for paper and pulp-based products.

» Growth in home-based PCs, development of disc storage, and other technologies eating into market for books.
» Further consolidation of paper and pulp-based manufacturers into global concerns.
» Chemicals suppliers required to address environmental issues.

Scenario 2: Migrating geese

» Manufacturers re-engineering organizations to focus on core competencies and high-added value activities. Transferring ownership and/or operation of plants to key suppliers.
» Consolidation of suppliers into first tier and second tier, reflecting moves in the auto industry.
» Accelerated transfer of manufacturing to low-cost economies.
» Increased pressure on second-tier suppliers to develop new products to improve process efficiency and reduce environmental impact.
» Access to capital for investment becoming increasingly tight as returns from the industry are low.

Scenario 3: Entrapped pheasant

» Environmental activists target paper and pulp processing, putting pressure on for "sustainability" in manufacture and recycling.
» Concerns increasing about corporate social responsibility, including the health and safety of staff and customers wherever located.
» Emergence of new players in the chemicals industry as scientific discoveries lead to alternative products.
» New players able to attack markets due to low cost base and nimble footedness.
» Emergence of more cost-effective and environmentally friendly mini-plants to service local needs.
» Fragmentation of the customer base for treatment products.
» Opportunities to help new entrants develop capabilities in process design, control, and maintenance.

Faced with these possible scenarios, these were Buckman's intentions.

» To accelerate the move to a consultancy business and away from commodity chemicals.

» An increase in innovative responses to changing customer need – a target of 25% of sales from products less than five years old (compared with 14%).
» Increased speed in decision making to enhance customer service – further empowerment of customer-facing staff and direct access within the organization to those who have "solutions."
» Increasing local presence alongside the facilities of global customers in order to meet their needs locally.
» Improved flow of information from the customer interface to all parts of the organization so as to unleash creativity and novel solutions.
» To develop a knowledge-transfer system to ensure complete access to company information for all staff.
» To use the IT infrastructure to support e-learning for all staff, any place, any time, up to and including PhD level.

The capabilities needs resulting from the 1990s scenarios are shown in Table 7.2.

Possible scenarios for paper and pulp processing – 2010

Scenario 1: Age of radical change

The Internet has taken off, providing access to most of the world's population which has a literacy age of 14+.

» In the wake of the Internet, and digital television and mobile telephony, the demise of the newspaper and glossy magazines in most countries.
» Publishing has become part of a much larger and more complex industry with a variety of enabling technologies, players, and delivery systems. Content providers are no longer necessarily publishers and publishers are not integrated communications companies either.
» Books have been largely consigned to the past.
» Many traditional applications of paper-based materials have been replaced by biodegradable plastics.
» Processing plants that survive are much larger, environment friendly, highly automated, and with remote sensing, diagnostics, and control.

Table 7.2   Capabilities needs resulting from the 1990s.

Knowledge and understanding	Technology	Management	Culture
Consultancy skills Develop personalized customer intimacy Enhanced expertise in process management Curiosity, creativity, and enthusiasm to contribute to innovation and new product development process World-class safety standards	Focus R&D on environment-friendly applications Development of open system for knowledge sharing accessible to all worldwide Develop system to disperse training and make it available to all	To make the knowledge-sharing system work to develop effective learning systems Understanding customers and competitors	Reward systems to strengthen sharing culture and effective deployment in problem situations Learning culture at individual, team, and organization levels Reinforce development of culture in line with values statement Reinforce safety culture

» The industry is consolidated, with ownership being distributed globally and decision making being increasingly centralized so as to benefit from economies of scale.

» The only surviving first-tier suppliers are knowledge-rich facilities management specialists and consultancies with access to supplies of commodity treatments shared across many industries.

Scenario 2: Evolution rather than revolution

» Despite all the earlier predictions about the Internet replacing the printed word, there has been a growth in newsprint, books, and other printed materials.

» The industry has largely relocated to a few centers where sustainable feedstocks are available. Development work on these sites is more or less continuous.
» Plants are highly automated.
» The supply industry is largely co-located on sites where processing takes place.
» A few centers of research excellence combining work on a range of technologies, and largely sponsored by manufacturers, compete to serve the industry. These are based on university campuses.
» The industry is generally highly competitive, with low margins. Chemical costs are essentially fixed.

Faced with these scenarios, these are Buckman's intentions.

» The company has already imported patents and other intellectual property rights (IPR) which will be developed further in partnership with several key universities and other specialist research-based organizations.
» In order to enable even more effective exploitation of its competencies, Buckman will continue to move toward total facilities management and away from its original manufacturing base. It will strengthen its partnership working with clients.
» To strengthen relationships with plant owners outside North and Central America and offer global service capability.
» The learning systems developed in the 1990s will be used to support training initiatives in both client organizations and those who are clients of clients.
» The best practice methodologies will be enhanced and shared more effectively through knowledge-sharing systems – technologies to enhance effective sharing across country locations will be implemented to increase plant profitability.
» Project teams will be strongly incentivized to improve client effectiveness, but reward systems will be designed also to strongly support sharing and learning.
» The company will more aggressively exploit its skills in facilities management to other processing industries.

The capabilities needs resulting from the 2000s scenarios are shown in Table 7.3.

Table 7.3 Capabilities needs resulting from the 2000s scenarios.

Knowledge and understanding	Technology	Management	Culture
Focus on niche area for R&D – bio-dispersants, which are environment friendly Understand process plant technologies Appreciate technology futures Broad-based view of process industry and stakeholders Business management	Tools for more effective collabora-tive working Best practice process control	Best practice process plant management processes and procedures Skills in managing highly competent knowledge workers Highly flexible organization structures Supply management Partnership management, including application of the 8 Company Business Management Standards management skills Bidding skills	Partnerships matter Respect for stakeholders Leadership of partnerships Innovation culture

ABB

Will the "giant" learn to tango?

This case study looks at the transformation process firms embark on to ensure sustained competitiveness into the future. How do successful, large multinationals transform themselves in midstream? The creation of ABB became a metaphor for the new model of the competitive enterprise, the answer to the changing economic map of Europe of the 1990s – the Europe of deregulated markets, globalization, and the emerging networked economy. Described in the past as "the dancing giant," ABB has reached a critical crossroads. Will it succeed in making the leap forward into the Internet-based future envisioned by Jörgen Centerman, who became the new CEO on January 1, 2001?

Here we review and discuss some of the key issues and critical milestones leading to ABB's organizational realignment – a transformation that, if successful, will irrevocably move it away from its traditional base in heavy engineering toward being a major global player in industrial automation and the Internet.

With its headquarters in Zürich, ABB is a Swedish-Swiss electrical and engineering giant forged through the 1987 merger of two venerable European companies, Asea of Sweden and Brown Boveri of Switzerland. Both companies had been flagships of industry in their respective countries for a century prior to the merger. The newly created Asea Brown Boveri quickly caught the fancy of the business world.

ABB and the "Barnevik era"

Indeed, ABB is a much-admired and much-studied company, thanks mainly to the prowess of Percy Barnevik, a charismatic and globetrotting dealmaker who put ABB together, ran the group for 10 years, and remains chairman of its non-executive board. Barnevik, a Swede, combined a no-nonsense approach with a willingness to innovate and take risks, notably the decisions to merge Asea with Brown Boveri, and to expand globally during the 1990s even while trying to keep a cohesive identity and culture.

Barnevik viewed ABB as an organization with three internal contradictions: wanting to be global and local, big and small, and radically decentralized with centralized reporting and control.[1] Success in resolving these contradictions, he noted, would be the basis for creating real organizational advantage. Barnevik, the big-vision, articulate leader who was consistently voted the most admired chief executive in Europe during his tenure, moved on in 1997 to oversee the holding company of Sweden's Wallenberg family. The company he left behind was described in *Forbes*[2] as "a tired manufacturing firm mired in nineteenth-century assets."

After Barnevik

Barnevik's act was a tough one to follow. Göran Lindahl, also a Swede, who succeeded Barnevik as chief executive in 1997, had inherited an ageing conglomerate. Dark clouds were appearing on the horizon. During Lindahl's first year in office, the net profit margin was down to 1.8%.[3] The new CEO enjoyed none of Barnevik's adulating press coverage. Indeed, the image often given of Lindahl in the early days of his tenure was that of the plodding engineer, closing factories and axing jobs, ever seeking opportunities to cut costs. But these measures did not impress the investors. Share prices dived.

Lindahl did more than cost-cutting, however. A number of acquisitions were engineered during his tenure, including one involving a new joint venture with France's Alstom. ABB Alstom became the world's largest power-generation company. The venture did not last long, however. Little more than a year after its formation, the two partners agreed to go their separate ways again. ABB used its cash resources to fund new ventures in e-commerce and related businesses. These moves were further steps along the path of change for ABB. In the previous few years it had begun to shed "old economy" businesses, including power generation and railway equipment, in favour of newer, information technology-related businesses.[4]

Lindahl's vision of the "new economy"

Lindahl's move to reduce his investments in power generation came as a shock in-house. Power generation had been ABB's bread and butter for 100 years. It marked the beginning of Lindahl's effort to move ABB away from its traditional expertise in heavy engineering toward industrial automation and the Internet.[5] Commenting on his gradual but deliberate move from power generation, Lindahl said:[6]

> "Engineers fall in love with certain businesses. That's our life. So, to get out of heavy assets like that, I couldn't talk about it. It was like swearing in church. [But] I just had to do it."

The industry was undergoing huge changes. Lindahl's vision was nothing less than that of transforming the sprawling multinational into an IT-based, services-oriented company, aided by novel applications of the Internet, that was to be capable of embracing and exploiting electronic means of spreading information as a way to cut internal administrative costs and to speed up the interaction between its employees and the company's customers and value chain.

Lindahl's vision underlined the profound impact that Internet-supported IT was beginning to have on the sector. Increasingly, the Web was seen to be more than a means to facilitate transactions involving the sale of goods and services. For ABB, the Internet was to be a communications pathway between the company and its customers - feeding the company's technology and trends know-how to corporate customers and learning, in return, about customers' ideas and picking up sales and orders. On the course chosen by Lindahl, ABB was to become the biggest user of e-business in its broadest form. The effort, according to Lindahl, was all about linking customers with what he called "ABB's brainpower" - the knowledge tucked away in the minds of its employees.

In late 2000, Lindahl announced his surprise decision to step aside as ABB's chief executive. The 55-year old CEO saw himself belonging to the "punch card generation" - the revolution, he felt, was better off in the hands of someone of the "IT generation." His successor was to be another Swede, 48-year-old Jörgen Centerman, head of ABB's large industrial-automation division, which accounted for about a third of the group's sales.

Centerman and the realigned ABB

On taking over as the new president and chief executive on January 1, 2001, Centerman moved quickly. On January 11, in a personal message to all employees, he announced his move to realign ABB global operations around customer groups. Centerman's initiative is a bold move. After all, ABB is an industrial giant with 160,000 employees and a presence in more than 100 countries around the globe. Corporations of that size normally do not possess the nimbleness and agility said to be needed in the Internet age.

The vision and the road ahead

Jörgen Centerman's vision is founded on the notion of "collaborative commerce" - linking suppliers, manufacturers, and customers using the Internet. In Centerman's view, "... the Internet will turn out to be a highly important tool [for] mass customization [tailor-made solutions to customer problems]."[7] Centerman has replaced the former four industrial divisions with four new customer segments, two product-based divisions, and a new arm to manage "corporate transformation."

The businesses will form a seamless front to the end users, with knowledge quickly transferring to where it can be useful across the group. "One voice and one face" to the customer is the new catchphrase. To balance ABB's "customer-centric" focus on its markets, New Ventures Ltd, a new business area, is to act as an incubator for new businesses. Centerman noted in his January 11 press release:[8]

> "New technologies continue to be a key driver of growth for us. Our R&D organization therefore remains critical. In addition, we're setting up New Ventures Ltd to identify, invest in, and to accelerate the development of new business opportunities."

He elaborated on the logic of the new structure:

> "The new structure allows us to grow faster by more easily delivering value to our customers. We have a unique, three-way combination. First, our superior domain expertise – that's our vast knowledge of our customers' market environment, their business processes, and success factors. Second, our world-class products and services. Third: collaborative commerce solutions that link the value chain all the way from suppliers through manufacturers to end users. This combination enables us to create comprehensive industrial IT offerings, with all products and services conforming to a common architecture.
>
> We are responding to a silent revolution in the market that is completely changing the business landscape. Faced with increasing complexity and speed – much of it driven by the Internet – our customers want clarity and simplicity. Our new structure will make it easier to do business with [us] and fully reflects our new vision of creating value and fueling growth by helping our customers become more competitive.
>
> This is what our customers request today to capitalize on technology advances and rapidly growing markets in order to be more competitive. This, in turn, will fuel growth for ABB. At the same time, it creates value for our shareholders and for the communities and countries where we operate."

Not unexpectedly, Centerman's change of course has jangled investors' nerves. ABB's share price has stumbled amid uncertainty about its ability to increase its profits. The investment community is watching closely.

Jörgen Centerman has clearly called for no less than what Senge has called "profound change." Profound change is revolutionary – it involves organizational change that "combines inner shifts in people's values, aspirations, and behaviours with "outer" shifts in processes, strategies, practices, and systems."[9] Above all, profound change demands *learning* – new dance steps and new rhythms. Centerman has called the new tune and ABB, the dancing giant, is now engaging in the "dance of change." The relentless pace and intensity of an Internet-driven networked global economy demands no less than that the "giant" learns to *tango*, in double time. Will ABB succeed? Centerman identifies two groups of managers: those who respond to his new ideas by saying "Yes, but . . ." and those who *say* "Why not?" Will Centerman succeed in winning over the first crowd for his revolution? Or is the critical question really about whether the new ABB boss' vision of an Internet-based future is correct? Perhaps the ultimate question is: Will the "giant" learn to tango?

A UK TELCOS PROVIDER[10]

Scenarios in strategic planning

A cellular telecommunications operator based in the United Kingdom has experienced phenomenal business expansion as a result of the introduction of longer-lived batteries for handsets, digital services, highly competitive offers (including large bundles of minutes at low average prices), and a high rate of adoption. However, profits have eluded the operator, even though the customers of the cellular operators are using their phones more often. They are becoming less and less valuable to the operators, as Fig. 7.1 shows.

Relative to revenues, the overall costs for the operator are increasing. Meanwhile, limiting the contract period to one year has contributed to an increase in the operator's churn rate by more than 7% since 1998, as Fig. 7.2 illustrates. Even though the telco has reduced its subsidies on the handsets, the cost of acquiring the most attractive customers and holding on to the best distributor outlets is going up, as Fig. 7.3 shows.

Over the past two years the price per minute of calls originating on a subscriber handset has been between 25p and 50p per minute. Analysis indicates that the average marginal cost to the operator is

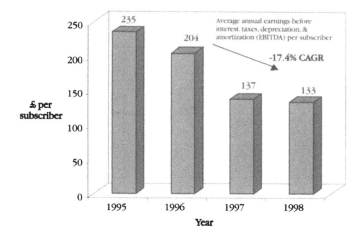

Fig. 7.1 Average annual earnings per subscriber.

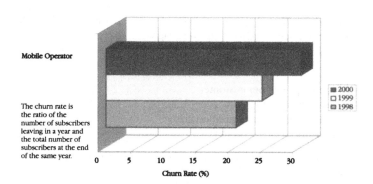

Fig. 7.2 Annual churn rates.

between 3p and 5p per minute and between 7p and 9p when long-run incremental expenses are included. This kind of disparity between price and marginal cost is unsustainable in a market with high fixed

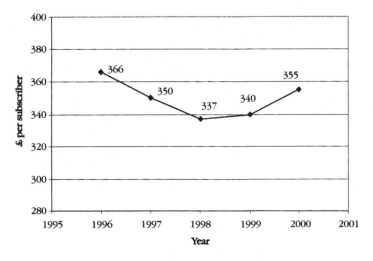

Fig. 7.3 The cost per new subscriber.

costs and this has led to a severe fall in the price per minute which the operator has been able to charge (see Fig. 7.4).

The challenges faced by the cellular telecommunications operator can be categorized as the following:

» declining profits per customer;
» increasing churn;
» increased customer acquisition costs;
» decreasing price for product.

In spite of these challenges the operator has grown its market share relative to the other operators (see Fig. 7.5).

Maintaining the lead

Management's challenge is to build from its current position in the marketplace and secure growth and success from directed planning and continued smart partnering. Top company executives sought to move into the uncharted future of such a dynamic industry with some

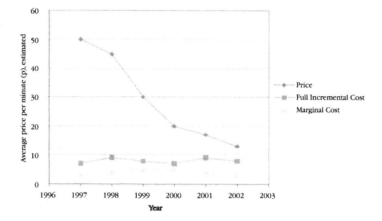

Fig. 7.4   The estimated average price per minute charged by the operator.

degree of considered forethought, and, in effect, anticipate how things might play out. They wanted the opportunity to mold the shape of things to come and the ability to develop a plan that considers all of the forces driving the UK cellular telecommunications market.

By doing so, they hoped to continue bringing value to the company at all levels of the business, as well as expand the company's position in the market. With those goals in mind, the management team set out to develop a compelling strategic plan that would provide focus, prioritization, and an overall roadmap for their UK business.

Using a disciplined approach, the team conducted a thorough debate about the most likely scenarios for the next three to four years and sought to ensure that the strategic objectives they developed were linked to a business plan that would deliver those objectives. To accomplish their goals, management used an outside consultancy to help them devise a scenario-based strategic planning process.

Looking forward from today, what futures may be most plausible for the industry? Will growth continue? What drivers will influence change, and how will they interact? The scenario planning experience addressed all of these questions while acknowledging the industry's current success and volatility, and determined the nature and influence

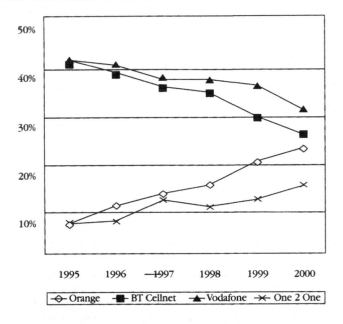

Fig. 7.5 The changing market share of operators.

of the drivers of the future. Importantly, the work recognized the need to develop practical business plans that could flow throughout the organization and produce immediate and visible results.

Overall the scenario process occurred in three distinct phases, each of which also contained a number of sub-phases (see Fig. 7.5 for a process map). Each of them involved a cross-section of management at all levels as well as key outside influencers. The overall phases were:

» scenario development: define the company's issues, objectives, and scenarios;
» analysis: identify the driving forces that would shape the industry and discuss this within the company;
» vision: predict and develop believable futures based on the key drivers, and build a shared vision with other company colleagues.

Scenario development: The key question or strategic decision that guides scenario planning and grounds it in reality must be established up front. For the telco, the issue was how to build and maintain a leadership position in a high-growth and rapidly changing industry. With that objective established, the scenario team identified key stakeholders who would have a role and interest in the strategic decision, and defined their potential impact. Such stakeholders included consumers, wholesalers and chains, competitors, and government regulators.

The first sub-phase within Phase 1, called the divergence stage, consisted of listening to the participants' various positions on the challenges facing the company. In the next sub-phase, called the emergence stage, internal and external experts addressed group members, broadening their knowledge of various subjects regarding the company. Finally, during the third sub-phase, the group engaged in a process of convergence, which started out with a broad number of alternatives and concluded with the three future scenarios, those judged the most relevant, novel, and substantial. (See Fig. 7.6.)

Analysis: The next task was to identify the driving forces that would shape the industry in the years ahead. The scenario team examined each of the following: political, economic, society, and technology.

They then cataloged more than 100 drivers, half of which the team considered predetermined by existing conditions. They identified those factors which they considered and labeled uncertain: industry consolidation, changes in regulation, and the failure to develop the next-generation technologies. Among the uncertainties, two-thirds were highlighted as critical in terms of their potential effect on the key strategic decision.

Once the critical uncertainties had been established, it was possible to group them under two broad themes of related/interconnected forces. Those themes formed the axes of a classic two-dimensional grid, and the quadrants of that grid then suggested areas in which industry futures might develop. In this case, the two broad themes emerging from the bundled critical uncertainties were failure of new technology and failure of the consumer to adopt the new products being sold by cellular telecommunications operators. The scenario team then established the degree of impact for each theme and graphically depicted the results.

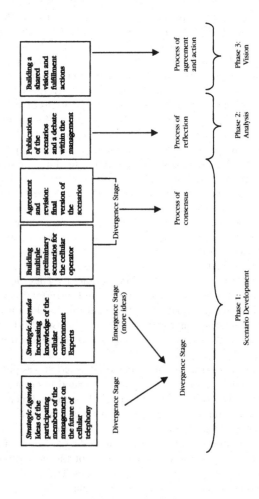

Fig. 7.6 The process of scenario building.

The scenario team then broke into groups to fully develop believable futures for each of the three quadrants in which industry futures were likely to develop. The group assigned memorable names to each theme and asked the teams to:

» write complete scenarios;
» identify the early warning signs that would signal the onset of a particular scenario or element;
» identify implications that would surface as a consequence of the unfolding scenario.

Various scenarios were identified.

1. Dangerous waters

In this scenario, several trends converge – consumer dissatisfaction with cellular telecommunications, lack of breakthrough products, unmet expectations for new products, and frustration among the distribution chain. The results are heightened scrutiny by regulatory and government bodies, and increased competitiveness within the industry itself.

In the "dangerous" future, larger companies succeed in containing costs and introduce one or two blockbuster products, while smaller companies struggle to stay afloat. Smart partnering, alliance formation, and mergers become keys to success. Additionally, consumers become more informed and consequently become major market drivers.

Major beacons of the "dangerous waters" scenario include:

» public concern over cost and quality of cellular telecommunications;
» outflow of capital;
» an increase in "hollow" good news.

Significant industry implications for the future are:

» industry consolidation;
» increased partnering.

2. Brave new world

Years of research and innovation begin to pay off in this scenario. Industry makes major breakthroughs in the systems. Third-generation technology comes of age; the pipeline fills with new products that promise to have a major impact on the way cellular technologies are used to connect producers and consumers.

Although this situation sounds ideal, the scenario includes factors that will stir up issues on many levels. At the societal level, escalating telecommunications costs and an increasing economic gap will create conflict between people with access to these services and people without.

In the "brave new world," companies will thrive by introducing breakthrough products and advance their positions by acquiring or collaborating with a whole variety of companies to further innovation. Competition will accelerate and the industry's growing attractiveness will lure conglomerates, such as Microsoft and GE, to purchase, merger, alliance, and partner their way in – thus creating a new industry.

Major beacons of the "brave new world" scenario include:

» progress in technology development;
» increased competitive pressure;
» new powers granted to Oftel, the regulator.

Significant industry implications for this future are:

» volume of innovations and increasing number of direct-to-consumer advertising campaigns will crowd available media space and limit companies' ability to capture a share of the available advertising "voice."

3. Sweet spot

This scenario represents the best of both worlds – rapidly expanding technological advances met with decreasing external control and rapid adoption of the new technology by consumers. Industry introduces innovative products that fulfill unmet communications needs.

The "sweet spot" future also stimulates cellular telecommunications companies to shift resources toward development of more leading-edge products. Companies with limited R&D resources will have to develop alliances and partnerships with other content companies and seek co-marketing opportunities for their successful products.

With a cache of innovative products and a public willing to pay for them, savvy marketing strategies – particularly to the consumer audience – will be especially important. Given the increased level of knowledge among consumers, public promotion will require more than just ads. Consumers will seek credible and comprehensive sources of information. Thus companies must also focus efforts toward recruiting and developing top-notch marketing teams with the capacity to optimize the opportunities that exist in this highly favourable scenario.

Major beacons of the "sweet spot" scenario include:

» an increase in patents for novel communications strategies;
» increased funding for established and start-up companies.

Significant industry implications for that future are:

» increased investment in R&D;
» expanded focus to include consumers and professionals;
» increased education of consumers about new product.

Planning strategies

Having defined the significant industry implications for each scenario, the operator's executives asked: "What strategies should our business adopt if the future horizon, driven by our individual scenario events, happens?" Although each scenario was designed to be discrete and independent, as were the business strategies flowing from each, the team set out to consolidate the scenario strategies into one set that was common to, and most compelling across, all of the futures. Such an action presumes that the "real" future of the industry will contain elements of all the scenarios, and that the consequent direction for the operator must be crafted in consideration. The company based its strategic business plan and the programs and actions that direct operations on a daily basis on the common set of strategies.

As a result of that work, planning at the operator has become an ongoing and integrated part of the business. The management team monitor constantly the major beacons mentioned before, and the signals have provided early warning that the future of the industry is shifting across the scenario quadrants described. Whether the "real" future of the industry is embedded within these scenarios is not the issue. Most likely, a combination of the events described, or others that the team failed to consider, will represent the field on which the cellular telecommunications industry will play in the future. The point, though, is that the scenario planning work gives planners the ability to anticipate the implications of unfolding futures and to rapidly convert them to strategic advantage. Such advantage ensures a robust presence well into the future, enabling the company to build an integrated vision, strategy, and action plan relevant to tomorrow.

A MALAYSIAN MANUFACTURING COMPANY[11]

Scenarios for future planning

In this case study we explore the possible futures facing LIH Berhad, a company which was incorporated in 1989 and which grew rapidly in the 1990s, manufacturing OEM plastic custom-molded products for assembly into a range of manufactured goods. Strategically LIH currently aims for:

» market leadership in those OEM markets in which it competes;
» 10% net profit growth rate annually over the next five years.

The company produces parts for the electronics, electrical, and automotive industries to meet customer specifications – 90% is sold into the local market, including 33% indirect exports through operations in free trade zones. Customers, mostly Japanese-based OEMs, normally provide design and product formulations, and even the molds used for making the parts are produced in the other home country of the OEM.

From 1987 to 1994, the export of electrical and electronic products grew at least 25% per annum. Up to 1996, Proton and other local car assemblers grew at a similar rate. Due to increasing labor shortages, rising wages, and a growing lack of competitiveness, the growth rate fell to 7.1% in 1997. In 1998, the pan-Asian economic crisis caused shock waves in Malaysia's manufacturing industry. While the severe depreciation of the ringgit helped to cushion erosion of some markets, the local automotive industry was not one of them.

Recently, improvements to molding machine reliability have come with the introduction of microprocessor control. Improved precision is opening up new applications, for example in very thin-walled parts and intricate electronic or plastic components. Progress is also being made in improving the properties of the chemical compounds used.

External environment – an overview

While regional economic crises have triggered political reform and leadership changes elsewhere in the Asean (Association of South East Asian Nations) region, Malaysia has remained relatively stable under the leadership of its prime minister Dr Mahathir. The government policy has for some time been aimed at encouraging foreign investment and trade. Local services such as legal, accounting, auditing, and tax are efficient, while a positive economic environment has created fiscal incentives, free trade zones, and flexible employment policies. A high level of domestic indebtedness, continuing strong credit growth, firmer interest rates, and the risks associated with an overbuilt property sector (to which banks are heavily exposed) are persistent concerns.

Malaysia is experiencing some of the problems associated with relentless economic growth, i.e. severe congestion, pollution, and reliance on foreign labor. The development of its educational infrastructure is high priority, with a 33% increase envisaged in the next national plan. The government is sensitive toward environmental quality and intolerant of international criticism. Since 1988, an environmental impact assessment is required from the government when setting up operations.

The OEMs are in a strong position to influence prices as most sales are large volume, there is strong competition among suppliers, and OEMs supply much of the expertise in research and product development. OEMs source globally and are able over time to switch to lower-cost regions. Supply of raw materials is highly concentrated and supply contracts tend to be in US dollars, so exchange fluctuations hurt profitability. The uniqueness of materials makes switching costs high.

Scenario 1 – "utility grade" (weak economic and weak environmental pressure)

In this scenario, after a promising start the government failed to introduce a comprehensive financial reform package along with the necessary prudent economic strategy, so little has been done to inspire investor confidence. Foreign investors have been put off by the government's constant intervention in the economy and capital controls have had a particularly profound effect. The corporate sector has failed to take the measures necessary to increase competitiveness.

The threat of pressure groups has not materialized; actions taken by government to recycle plastic waste have dissipated the environmentalists' heat. The fluctuating economy has caused cyclical retrenchments and even company closures. Investment in training and new technology has been so curtailed that the long-term viability of the industry is in question.

Scenario 2 – "aim grade" (strong economic and weak environmental pressure)

Five years ago, in response to the deep financial crisis, the government took the necessary severe measures to rectify the situation. After considerable initial pain, the economy recovered quickly and returned to steady growth. Corporations are healthy again. Currency stability has been achieved.

The Malaysian government has continued to promote free trade, currency convertibility and free capital flows, deregulation, and competition based on free markets, and the country is seen as a good place to invest. Consistently lower interest rates have enabled forward planning. Stability in consumer confidence has maintained a growth in domestic demand. Manufacturers have adopted a proactive strategy in tackling the problem of plastic wastes by forming task forces with the environmentalists and have worked toward solutions on a number of environmental issues. Plastic is still the cheapest material for OEM products and therefore demand has grown and Malaysia has remained at the forefront of production.

Scenario 3 – "off spec" (strong economic and strong environmental pressure)

In this scenario, Malaysia's economy is similar to that in scenario 2 but there is a strong and growing environmental pressure against the consumption of plastic products. Public awareness and concern has grown about a wide range of environmental issues, including global warming, deforestation, and impacts on health such as cancer risks.

Despite intense lobbying from industry, the environmental legislation introduced is regarded as punitive and leading to an inevitable decline in competitiveness. Traditional manufacturers have been slow to respond by failing to seek out new materials, new processes, and increasing recycling efforts. But now the threat of new entrants is high due to the existence of eco-efficient substitute products, such as biodegradable plastic products.

Action scenarios

The first step in using these scenarios was to identify the key business decisions required to achieve success and to minimize the risk of failure in each scenario. (See Table 7.4.)

Table 7.4 Action scenarios.

Scenario 1 – "Utility grade" (weak economy and weak environmental pressure)	Scenario 2 – "Aim grade" (strong economy and weak environmental pressure)	Scenario 3 – "Off-spec" (strong economy and strong environmental pressure)
How to cope with a contraction in demand for plastic parts?	Can LIH cope with the expansion of the market? And how best to manage growth?	Can LIH cope with the expansion of the market? And how best to manage growth?
How to take advantage of the weak environmental pressure?	How to take advantage of the weak environmental pressure?	How to sustain competitive edge given strong environmental pressure?

Whether to exploit existing segments at home and abroad or to move into other segments or related areas?

How to sustain competitive edge in the conditions suggested by the scenarios?

Can LIH compete on cost against the competitors if focus differentiation through features is no longer in demand? Can the company develop a new generation of products which meet the changed needs of the consumer?

Will the plastic injection molding industry still be an attractive industry to be in? Are there related industries which offer better long-term prospects?

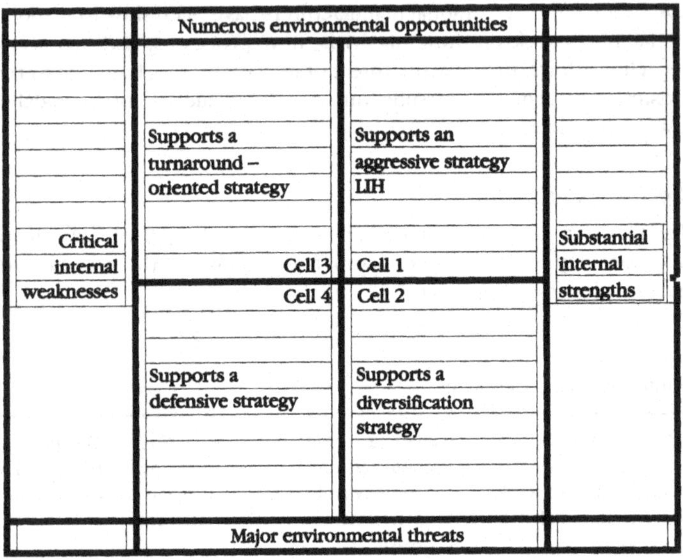

	Numerous environmental opportunities		
	Supports a turnaround – oriented strategy	Supports an aggressive strategy LIH	
Critical internal weaknesses	Cell 3	Cell 1	Substantial internal strengths
	Cell 4	Cell 2	
	Supports a defensive strategy	Supports a diversification strategy	
	Major environmental threats		

Fig. 7.7 SWOT analysis.

Current internal analysis

Following a SWOT analysis the LIH board considered the current position as being in cell 1 (Fig. 7.7), seen as the most favorable situation. There are several opportunities and numerous strengths that encourage pursuit of these opportunities. The executive decided on aggressive strategies/growth-oriented strategies to exploit the favorable match within each of the five-year scenarios.

From the detailed SWOT analysis the board concluded that the most important areas of strength were the advanced production technology and quality control/assurance, and that these were the core competencies which LIH should concentrate on exploiting within the three scenarios. But the analysis also led to the recognition that the low utilization rate of fixed assets and the weak financial position were the main threats to progressing the business.

Strategic options

The following strategic issues were then addressed:

» What would LIH do if . . .?
» How does each scenario explain what is happening out there?
» How to react in each scenario?
» What other options are there?
» What is the customer value created?
» What is the nature of the competitive advantage exploited?
» What core competencies are used, and what is their mutually rein-
forcing configuration?
» What is the positive feedback loop driving growth?

The influence diagram shown in Fig. 7.8 was used to represent the
essence of the underlying factors for the success of LIH. The diagram
shows the nine key success factors (as numbered) identified for a plastic
injection molding company in this industry. Two core competencies,
namely quality control/assurance and advanced production technology,
are highlighted. Overall, LIH is striving to have special appeal toward
industrial buyers, focusing on differentiation by maintaining the lead
in quality and technology, and providing superior customer service.
Therefore the current strategy of LIH is focus differentiation.

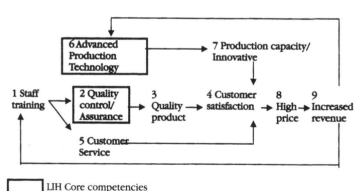

Fig. 7.8   Influence diagram for LIH (present).

Three generic strategy approaches to outperform other firms in an industry were considered.

» Striving for an overall low-cost leadership in the industry.
» Striving to create and market unique products for varied customer groups through differentiation.
» Striving to have special appeal toward one or more groups of consumers or industrial buyers, focused on their cost or differentiation concerns.

The three generic strategies were assessed to decide ways to sustain or improve the competitive position of LIH under each scenario, as shown in Table 7.5. Each was rated according to the extent to which each generic strategy addressed the key issues arising from the scenario. Adding up the individual scores leads to the choice of cost-focus strategy for all the scenarios.

Table 7.5 Scenario/alternatives strategy matrix.

Option	Scenario 1 – "Utility grade" (weak economy and weak environmental pressure)	Scenario 2 – "Aim grade" (strong economy and weak environmental pressure)	Scenario 3 – "Off -spec" (strong economy and strong environmental pressure)
Alternative strategies			
Concentrated growth	10	10	10
Market development	9	9	9
» Regional	(i)	(i)	(i)
» International	(ii)	(ii)	(ii)
» Third world countries (loose environmental regulation	–	–	(iii)
Product development	8	8	8
Innovation			
» Environmental protection product	–	–	7
Vertical integration	7	7	6
Concentric diversification	6	6	6

NOTES

1 Taylor, W. (1991) "The logic of global business: an interview with ABB's Percy Barnevik," *Harvard Business Review*, March–April.
2 Morais, R.C. (1999) "After Barnevik, better," *Forbes Global*, August 23.

3 Morais, R.C. (1999) op cit.

4 Marsh, P. (2000) "Not every marriage is made in heaven: when Alstom and ABB split, the market opted for power over technology," Companies & Finance: International, *Financial Times*, April 1.

5 Marsh, P. (2000) "Welding metal to the Internet," *Financial Times*, October 30.

6 Morais, R.C. (1999) op cit.

7 Marsh, P. (2000) op cit.

8 ABB Corporate Communications.

9 Senge, P. (1999) *The Dance of Change*, p. 5. Currency-Doubleday, New York.

10 We are extremely grateful to Raj Kumar, an alumnust of Henley Management College, for the development of this case.

11 We thank Foong Wing Keong, an alumnust of Henley Management College, who worked on this case with the managing director and the executive team, and was prepared to share the outputs. Background information was gleaned about the external environment and the plastics industry from a range of public sources such as government reports, newspapers, and articles.

Key Concepts and Thinkers

This chapter is about key concepts and thinkers in the field of future proofing. The reader is introduced to a variety of concepts that help in defining the field, and will learn about a number of key theorists.

INTRODUCTION

Future proofing is a strategic process aimed at mapping a way forward for the organization which takes into consideration the best possible information and opinions about the future, developing a vision for the company informed by this world view and then working out broad-brush plans to take the company in the desired direction. By adopting a scenario planning process the organization can recognize alternative possible futures and then start to map routes which minimize the likelihood of the unexpected impacting on the business. The key concepts are the strategy process itself and the competencies assessment as part of this, the recognition of technology futures and their impact on the business, scenario planning, and organizational learning – the process of embedding a futures view of the organization into daily working practices.

EMERGENT VS. PLANNED STRATEGY

The firm's current strategic position and its disposition toward change are closely linked. Real-time strategy is not nearly as static or rigid as one might be tempted to infer from traditional annals on strategic planning. Real strategy is not enacted in five-year planning cycles. In reality, we do not find strategy "purely by plan." We know that business environments are dynamic; markets and competitive environments in particular are moving targets. Consequently, no one would realistically expect to formulate a long-term strategic plan and follow it mindlessly.[1]

Strategic management thinker Walter Kiechel,[2] who for many years wrote about strategy for *Fortune* magazine, once made reference to a study that suggested that only about 10% of formulated strategies got implemented (a figure which according to management guru Tom Peters is "wildly inflated"). One of the great thought leaders of our time in this area has been the Canadian Henry Mintzberg, a professor of strategy at McGill University in Montreal. Mintzberg has been a strong proponent of the "learning school," which views strategy formation as an emergent process. The learning school has triggered a disturbing debate within the school of strategic management focused on who really is the architect of strategy and where in the organization strategy formation actually takes place; how deliberate and conscious the strategy process really is; and whether the separation of strategy formulation and implementation really is sacrosanct.[3]

Indeed, we find that firms develop strategic plans for the future while evolving patterns out of their past. The first is referred to as "intended strategy," the latter as "emergent strategy."[4,5] We find that in fast-changing environments, successful strategies tend to emerge from a multiple stream of decisions that originate in various parts of the organization (Fig. 8.1).

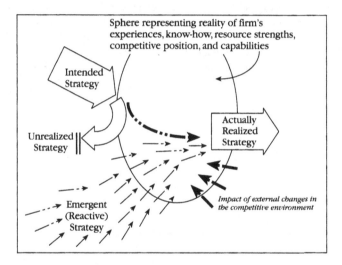

Fig. 8.1 Deliberate and emergent strategies. (Source: Adapted from Mintzberg *et al.* (1998) *Strategy Safari*, The Free Press, London.)

Mintzberg argues that *realized* strategy is the combined outcome of *deliberate* and *emergent* strategy. The part of the *intended* (or *planned*) strategy that is, in fact, realized is *deliberate* strategy. Much of the realized strategy, however, emerges as a result of events that were not part of the intended strategy. This part is called the *emergent* strategy.

Indeed, we find the notion of an idealized, planned, and deliberate strategy process probably as much a myth as the notion of the reflective, systematic, strategic planning activities of managers. Mintzberg[6] reminds us here also that managers' "activities are characterized by brevity, variety, and discontinuity, and ... [managers] are strongly oriented to action and dislike reflective activities." Strategy as an outcome of this management action is consequently more appropriately seen to emerge as a pattern reflecting a stream of actions over time.

The pattern itself can be evaluated only after the event. It will reveal how much of the actually realized strategy was intended, how much unintended. Emergent strategy manifests itself in a variety of ways. At Intel Corporation, it surfaced – in the words of Andy Grove, Intel's CEO at the time – as strategic dissonance, a divergence between the statements of senior management and the actual actions taken by its employees.

STRATEGIC INFLECTION AND EMERGENT STRATEGY AT INTEL CORPORATION

Former Intel CEO Andy Grove[7] talks about *strategic inflection points* and their implications for emergent strategies; how firms, when in the midst of coping with a strategic inflection point, often fall into the trap of saying one thing and doing another. This, for Grove, is clear evidence of *strategic dissonance*. In recalling how Intel exited the memory business, he relates how the process of emergent strategy that ultimately led to the company's shift to microprocessor production began with various project leaders, marketing managers, and plant supervisors, who through their daily work were busy refocusing Intel's strategy by shifting resources from memories to microprocessors some two years before top management woke up to this reality.

Intel's top management might have been "fooled by our strategic rhetoric," Grove confessed, "but those on the front lines could see that we had to retreat from memory chips ... People formulate strategy with their fingertips. Our most significant strategic decision was not made in response to some clear-sighted corporate vision but by the marketing and investment decisions of frontline managers who really knew what was going on."[8]

CORE COMPETENCIES AND CAPABILITIES

The notion of core competencies was introduced by C.K. Prahalad and Gary Hamel in their seminal, award-winning *Harvard Business Review* papers "Strategic intent"[9] and "The core competence of the corporation."[10] These papers resonated well with academics and management practitioners alike. This was not only because of their persuasiveness, crafting, and style, but also because of the timeliness of the idea. The papers' immediate and unusually broad resonance drew on the readiness of the management world for this message. Up to that point, corporate strategy had been seen largely as a cash flow and controlling problem. Practitioners and academics were ready for a view of strategy that emphasized the importance of technology, skill, and synergy for future competitiveness.[11]

These papers were followed by the authors' bestseller *Competing for the Future*[12] in which Hamel and Prahalad took the notion of competencies even further, showing how firms can build competitive advantage into the future – pre-empt the future – by developing the appropriate industry foresight necessary to proactively shape industry evolution. Core competencies help the firm to create and deliver differential value to the firm's customers in this scenario.

Hamel and Prahalad's concept of core competencies has the following four key elements.[13]

1 *Corporate span*. Core competencies span the entire business, not just a single business unit, supporting the differential value potential of several products or businesses.
2 *Temporal dominance*. Competencies are stable and evolve over relatively long periods of time (this can be 5–10, or even more, years). They cannot be acquired "overnight."
3 *Learning by doing*. Competencies represent accumulated, collective learning in the organization. Futhermore, they do not diminish with use, rather – as with strategically relevant organizational knowledge, which they are in fact a form of – they are enhanced as they are applied and shared.

4 *Competitive locus.* Hamel and Prahalad conceived the firm as a portfolio of core competencies and disciplines, as opposed to inter-product competition, and it is essentially concerned with the acquisition of skills.

Core competencies are made up of bundles of core or key capabilities and these, in turn, are made up of clusters of individual knowledge sets and skills, experience, and insight, much of which resides in the tacit realm. Capabilities are understood to be bundles of constituent skills and technologies – rather than single, discrete skills or technologies – that create disproportionate value for the customer, differentiate its owner from competitors, and allow entrance to new markets.[14] Needless to point out, capabilities represent an accumulation of learning over time.

A firm's portfolio of knowledge-driven capabilities is a dynamic entity; it must be managed in the context of the firm's rapidly changing environment. Firms must therefore focus as much on their future portfolio of capabilities as on their current stock of capabilities. A thorough identification and analysis of a firm's core competencies portfolio requires considerable effort and time. Ideally it is carried out within a multidisciplinary team and on an ongoing basis. Generally, the time frame and scope of the firm's industry will dictate the frequency of analysis.[15]

TECHNOLOGY ROADMAPPING/QFD

Probably one of the most advanced industry-wide technology roadmapping exercises is undertaken in the semi-conductor industry.[16] In bringing together representatives from the Semiconductor Industry Association (USA), the European Electronic Component Association, the Electronic Industries Association of Japan, the Korean Semiconductor Industry Association, and the Taiwan Semiconductor Industry Association, the roadmapping exercise unites the world's leading expertise. But why would competitors be willing to share their insights in this way?

The semiconductor has its origins in technical investigations initiated in the 1940s. But it was only in the late 1960s that the semiconductor industry as we know it today emerged. The technology has moved so far since then that the International Technology Roadmapping for Semi Conductors Group (ITRS) sees it as difficult for any single company to support the progressively increasing R&D spend necessary both to evolve the current technology and to develop a set of new dimensions usable to set the limits of current technology. The members of ITRS accept that much of the R&D effort needs to be in the "pre-competitive domain." One of the aims of the roadmapping efforts is to give the industry overall a common reference and to encourage co-operative investment and a more uniform sharing of the R&D costs.

The ITRS roadmap classifies challenges into two groups.

» Relatively near-term that need to be met by "technology solutions" currently under development
» No "known solutions" (with reasonable confidence). These are classified as "red" and signify that progress might end if breakthroughs are not achieved or some "work-around" developed.

The ITRS is useful as an illustration of the process for constructing the roadmap. Credibility is based on the standing of the contributing experts and their knowledge of R&D. The International Technology Working Group (ITWG) overseeing the process includes chipmakers, equipment and materials suppliers, government, and universities. In addition, feedback is sought from sub-group meetings as well as public roadmap workshops. The ITWG oversees the work of two types of sub-group – those which focus on sub-activities of the process from design/process/test/package, and those which have a "cross-cut" focus, i.e. environmental, health/safety, defect reduction, metrology, and modeling/simulation.

Overall roadmap technology tables are used to summarize high-level technology requirements based on what is seen as a compelling economic strategy to maintain a high rate of advancement in integrated circuit technologies. These tables indicate current best estimates of the timing of introduction, possibly broken down into research, development, prototyping, and manufacturing, although it may be confined to year of introduction, which is the estimate of the point at which the technology will be "at the leading-edge of ramp to volume manufacturing."

Industry technology roadmaps can be useful in informing specific businesses which then can take the mapping process further to look at their own development needs. Within firms such as Motorola, the roadmapping process is ongoing. So their processes are well established and documented. But for those less familiar with the process, the means for producing the roadmap need to be thought through carefully, as do the ways in which it will be used. Access to expertise and good facilitation of the process is clearly important, and tools such as QFD and an innovation matrix can be useful adjuncts to the process. By focusing on functional requirements of customers QFD is able to then translate these into technical features of the product. Here timescales and process technologies are not considered in detail. This can serve as a simpler starting point than with a full roadmap. The next stage – the technology roadmap – can build on this output by either adopting a technology push or a market pull perspective. This either shows others what technology is required to meet product functionality or else how technology will make possible different product functionality.

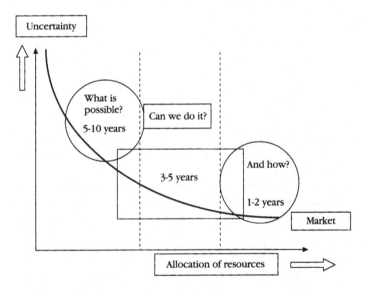

Fig. 8.2 The blue box model from Groenveld.

Philips17 has used a tool – the Blue Box Model – in which the uncertainty of product feasibility and commitment to resource allocation is shown (see Fig. 8.2). This is the basis of the innovation matrix (Fig. 8.3), which shows the technical uncertainty, and hence risks, against the requirement of availability. This matrix identifies particular short-term needs with unproven technology – problems. Also areas where technology, while available, is not needed for a considerable time – premature R&D spend and areas where the business has access to proven technology essential for the mid-term – a desirable situation.

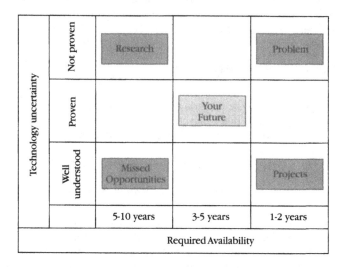

Fig. 8.3 The innovation matrix from Groenveld.

Technology roadmapping may then include the following.

» Mapping the innovation matrix onto the product matrix; identifying gaps and establishing actions.
» Reviewing the portfolio of technologies and assessing the overall balance of risks.
» Reviewing the product portfolio to assess possible gaps within the future portfolio if technologies are not available within the timeframe.

The relevance of platform innovation is stressed by Marc Meyer and Paul Mugge.[18] They argue that a robust platform strategy is a "common-sense way for a firm to leverage technology into new markets and at the same time reduce per-unit costs." Platforms in their terminology are "simple pictures of major sub-systems and interfaces between these sub-systems." Platforms can be readily identified in assembled physical products but also exist in non-physical products such as software and services. By focusing on platforms and their sub-systems, the impact of new technologies on the overall system for product service can be more readily recognized and future proofed.

SCENARIO PLANNING

> "Learning how to use scenario thinking can be likened to success in learning how to ride a bicycle – practice is essential. Once you have mastered it, you pick it up quickly, even after periods of under-use."
> *Bill Weinstein, "The use of scenario thinking," in Garratt, B.*
> *(ed.),*
> *Developing Strategic Thought, McGraw Hill, 1995*

There is little doubt about the power of scenario building to aid strategic thinking within organizations. However, despite the impact of the technique within Shell, it is still relatively little used generally. Among those tools most used by executives it comes well down the list compared with benchmarking, customer satisfaction measures, and pay-for-performance, but as a technique it has a relatively low defection rate, suggesting that those who use it continue doing so.[19]

The impact that scenarios can have is highlighted by Kees van der Heijden,[20] a former Shell executive who now consults and teaches. He points out that most strategic planning tools are backward looking or are focused on internal problems; scenarios on the other hand are forward looking and external. "Scenarios increase the organization's capability to more skillfully observe its environment, leading to more robust long-term organizational learning." It is seen as shifting strategic thinking from reactive to proactive and from internal to external.

The reason for Shell introducing the process was to enable planning at a strategic level without having to predict things that everyone knew were unpredictable. Based on experiences at Shell, van der Heijden concludes that:

» scenarios led to projects and decisions that were more robust under a variety of alternative futures;
» scenarios did not produce definitive decisions, rather they yielded information relevant for decision making;
» scenarios resulted in better thinking about the future because they required in-depth consideration of the driving forces in the business environment;
» people who practiced scenario planning found themselves interpreting information from the environment differently than others around them.

Aries de Geus[21] clearly felt that the use of scenarios led to a focus on the company's decision-making processes in such a way that later led to the recognition that decision making is a learning process. Reflection can lead to new patterns and trends being identified that were not perceived before, and to the formulation of what are described as new mental models or theories about how the observed phenomena operate. These new models are then applied and tested in the real world and the outcomes observed. New reflection leads to revision of the mental models. As this process is largely a group process, the model testing and review is a collective activity.

For individuals, learning through scenarios results from improved cognition through organizing multiple fragments of information into a coherent "story." Individuals involved in the process are forced to set aside personal biases and consider alternatives, thereby improving perception. For the group, scenario building focuses individuals on examining strategic issues from an organizational perspective and is thus a means by which collectively people start to align their individual mental models.

So if scenarios have this considerable potential, why is the process not embedded into the strategic decision processes of most organizations? One reason may well come out of descriptions of its use within Shell. Clearly the effort put in was enormous: teams of high-level people working for months at a time; interviews with thousands of people, both internal and external; a major communications and sharing exercise in using the eventual output of the building process. All of this may be seen as a major attempt to change the culture from a reactive approach to one which is more proactive. But such initiatives require a concerted effort over considerable time. In the case of petroleum companies where the time horizon for bringing on stream new oil reserves is many years, this may be justified. Many executive committees would probably not consider dedicating so much resource to something which, while demonstrated to have benefitted a number of companies, may well not work on their own. The process is also challenging for executive committees because it has the potential to expose any lack of understanding they have of the business in which they operate, the drivers for change, and the often implicit business models they hold but which channel decision processes.

The process of scenario building, however, does not have to be anywhere near as elaborate as that used by Shell. Clearly the more extensive and all-embracing the exercise, the greater the comfort that can be drawn from the output. Credibility is gained through consultation and involvement of leading experts. For many organizations this is not feasible, but nevertheless scenarios can still be powerful tools. Other writers illustrate the use of scenario building which is much less elaborate, including work reported by van der Heijden. Considerable work can be achieved even in a one-day executive workshop if the participants are well prepared and the workshop is run skillfully.

The point in time at which scenario planning is introduced to the organization may also be important in its eventual acceptance. Schoemaker[22] suggests that scenarios are most beneficial when the organization:

» has experienced, or is about to experience, significant change;
» faces great uncertainty that is straining managers' efforts to predict or adjust;
» has difficulty thinking strategically or has a low quality of strategic thinking;
» has a difficult time perceiving or generating new opportunities;
» requires a common language and framework to advance change;

» includes constituents with strong differences of opinion, many with merit.

Another factor which may lead organizations to fail to drive home the benefits of the scenario exercise is the way in which the output is used. Storytelling is an important aspect in the application of scenarios in influencing organizational thinking. The construction of good quality and memorable stories is part of the art of the scenario builder. The stories have to be plausible to gain credibility within the organization at large. But those constructing the stories need to recognize how their own bias will impact the storyline they develop. That is not to suggest a uniform style of story, but considerable thought needs to be given to how the story will be presented and the impact it might have. Above all, the stories need to disturb the listener. If they fail in this they will soon be forgotten and will not have the desired effect of galvanizing thinking, decision making, and action.

Great care also needs to be taken in selecting those to present the stories. Unless they themselves have credibility – "having been there, done it and got the tee-shirt (or battle scars) to prove it" – the stories are unlikely to be well received.

So there is undoubtedly the potential to extend the use of scenario building within organizations, not only as a useful mechanism to increase organizational learning but also to engage the organization in developing foresight. The importance of the latter is stressed by Hamel and Prahalad[23] as having the goal to "build the best possible assumption base about the future and thereby develop the prescience needed to proactively shape industry evolution." Mintzberg[24] acknowledges with a health warning that, when looking at the external environment, "some of the softer techniques, such as scenario building, may be of use ... not to predict, but simply to interpret and clarify for managers what seems to be going on out there."

On a final note, Islei *et al.*,[25] a group of UK experts in decision sciences, stress that techniques for evaluating future scenarios have to be designed with care. A too-narrow focus on financial aspects can stifle opportunities; a too-narrow focus on technological innovation can damage a company's future. Too simple a system can result in distortions; too complicated a system can be unworkable. Additionally, there is no single methodology that can be applied across all industries and all types of research.

STEVE DENNING OF THE WORLD BANK

Storytelling in organizations

Good organizational stories have five key characteristics:

Endurance (the stories go on through decades);

Salience (they have punch and emotional power);

Sense making (they explain something);

Comfort (the story rings true to something people have experienced);

Authenticity (people trust the storyteller and believe the story).

Stories can be used in organizations to stimulate change, to convince people of what you want them to believe, to gain commitment and loyalty, and to transfer knowledge. Some people are natural storytellers, but it is a technique everyone can learn.

Quoted from a talk given to the Knowledge Management
Forum at Henley in June, 2001

ORGANIZATIONAL LEARNING – KEY CONCEPTS AND THOUGHT LEADERS

"Companies could act according to the economic definition of success when managers felt that they were in control of their world. But rare is the manager who feels in control of today's turbulent environment. Therefore, to cope with a changing world, any entity must develop the capability to shift and change, to develop new skills and attitudes: in short, the capability to learn."

Arie de Geus, The Living Company, p. 27

Argyris and Schon[26] set the scene for the high level of interest in organizational learning. But it was Peter Senge, in *The Fifth Discipline*,[27] who gave the topic a degree of practicality, thereby launching it into the mainstream. The principal drivers of interest in the learning organization stem from the move to the knowledge-based economy along with emerging hypercompetition. But Denton[28] also identifies as a driver the disillusionment of managers with a paradigm that has not coped with past changes, let alone future ones.

Organizational learning and the learning organization are used interchangeably, but "organizational learning" is really an action or process, whereas "the learning organization" is an end state or a product of the process.

A basic assumption is that there is no learning without action. Action learning relies on the concept of "doubt" and "error detection and correction" in a process, such as:

» an individual takes action;
» an unexpected outcome creates a doubt (error detection);
» thought ensues about why the problem may have occurred;
» further action is taken to test the conclusions of thought (error correction);
» a new problem, or unexpected result transpires (error detection);
» learning has occurred and knowledge has been created;
» this is an ongoing and iterative process – there is no "final settlement."

Learning is deemed to have occurred because the individual has modified beliefs and understanding about what and why things happen the way they do. Once learning has occurred, the end product can be classed as knowledge. Knowledge may be represented by:

» strategies of action – based on values and assumptions;
» values that govern choice of strategies – the beliefs that make C desirable;
» underlying assumptions – "world model" that makes it plausible that action A will produce consequence C.

It has been suggested[29] that information distribution, and therefore organizational learning, depends on:

» members routing information to one another;
» minimal delays in such routing;
» minimal distortion in such routing.

If the learning process is concerned with, among other things, assumptions, values, and beliefs, then the starting point for any given learning event will be different for every individual, depending on their history and experience. Information interpretation, then, introduces the theme of diversity and conflict to organizational learning (highlighted by both Senge and Huber).

Huber, from the University of Texas in Austin, suggests there are four factors that affect the extent to which interpretation of new information is shared.

1 Cognitive maps: the individual's prior mental model of the world dictates the manner in which the information is labeled or framed.
2 Media richness: determines the extent to which information is given common meaning by sender and receiver.
3 Information overload: interpretation across organizational units is less effective if the information to be interpreted exceeds the unit's capacity to process the information adequately.
4 Unlearning: a process by which learners discard knowledge (and thereby decrease their range of potential behaviours).

Senge describes learning disabilities. He focuses on the failure of people and organizations to look beyond their immediate time and space horizons during the process of error detection and correction. Building on this idea, Fiol and Lyles,[30] who at the time were researching at the University of Illinois, Champaign, in the USA, refer to four contextual factors that may inhibit organizational learning.

1 Culture – the shared beliefs, norms, and ideologies that influence organizational action taking.
2 Strategy – the boundary to decision making and interpretation of the environment that determine the breadth of actions available for implementing it.
3 Structure – centralized structures reinforce past behaviours while decentralized structures "reduce the cognitive workload of the individuals, thereby facilitating the assimilation of new patterns and associations."
4 Environment – if the environment is too complex, overload occurs and learning is impaired; if there is too much stability, there is little inducement to learn or change.

Argyris and Schon refer to the face-saving activities of individuals that inhibit error detection and correction. Human rationality can also be a barrier to organizational learning since rationality does not value experimentation and "abhors mistakes" – one of the key elements of error detection and correction. The rational model also denigrates the importance of values, one of the theoretical building blocks of organizational learning.

In the words of Argyris and Schon, "organizational learning is only useful (to the organization) when it stimulates inquiry that leads to:

» improved performance of a task;
» restructuring of the values and criteria that define what improved performance means;
» enhancing the learning capability of an organization to achieve improved task performance and restructuring of values and criteria."

They qualify the usefulness of organizational learning by emphasizing the need for "productive learning."

> Organizational defensive routines are defined as "the actions and policies, enacted within an organizational setting, that are intended to protect individuals from experiencing embarrassment or threat, while at the same time preventing individuals, or the organization as a whole, from identifying the causes of the embarrassment or threat in order to correct the relevant problem."
>
> Argyris, C. and Schon, D., *Organizational Learning*, p. 99.

KNOWLEDGE AND KNOWLEDGE MANAGEMENT

Knowledge, not capital assets, is increasingly becoming the source of wealth in today's global economy. Not only is this true for the obviously knowledge-intensive high-technology sectors, but traditional manufacturing and utilities industries are also recognizing that using knowledge about customers to provide improved services can build a formidable competitive edge in fast-moving markets.

Information and communications technologies have been a major driver behind the rediscovery of knowledge and its importance for building competitiveness. Technology has made it possible for people to share information and knowledge across traditional boundaries imposed by organizational structures and geography. Yet in spite of all the advances in information and communication technologies we have seen in the past several decades, and their capability to change the way we create, transfer, and use knowledge, there is growing recognition that technology has its limitations, particularly in the case of facilitating the transfer of some forms of knowledge that depend on face-to-face encounters. Knowledge of this type is known as tacit knowledge. Arguably, it is the most strategically relevant and valuable form of knowledge for the firm.

Two of the most influential thinkers in the knowledge management area, Ikujiro Nonaka and Hirotaka Takeuchi, introduced the notion of the different forms of knowledge in an article by Nonaka[31] that appeared in the *Harvard Business Review* in 1991 and the jointly authored *The Knowledge Creating Company*[32] in 1995. The book, which has sold nearly 40,000 copies, is still widely viewed as a landmark work in the field of knowledge management. One of its important contributions is the distinction between explicit and tacit knowledge.

Enabling Knowledge Creation,[33] a sequel, extends Nonaka and Takeuchi's notions by describing practical "enablers" for the creation of organizational knowledge. Knowledge, the authors assert, cannot be managed, only enabled. The term "management," they explain, implies control of processes that may be inherently uncontrollable. Managers need to support the creation of knowledge creation by providing the appropriate enablers – the overall set of organizational activities that positively affect knowledge creation.

Since the mid-90s there has been an increased focus on knowledge as an intangible asset. The notion of organizational knowledge as an intangible asset has thrown traditional accounting into a real dilemma. One of the greatest challenges facing firms today focuses on the question of how to account for the gap between its balance sheet and its market value. The gap represents the bulk of the company's true value – its organizational knowledge in the form of product innovation, employee morale, patents and trademarks, and other intangible, hard-to-grasp assets – which never appear in an annual report. Traditional accounting methods that have served over past centuries no longer capture the essence of a firm's real value.

A number of thought leaders have made important contributions to our understanding of knowledge as an intellectual asset. Karl Erik Sveiby's *The New Organizational Wealth*[34] has been instrumental in helping managers understand how to identify the appropriate indicators for their company's intangible assets, including the various knowledge contributions of employees, customers, and suppliers. Thomas Stewart,[35] another influential writer, focused on the human, structural, and customer components of intellectual capital, showing how large firms such as General Electric, Hewlett-Packard, and Merck & Co. have managed intellectual capital to improve performance.

Leif Edvinsson,[36] former director of intellectual capital at Skandia, the Swedish financial services company, has been another influential thinker in the area of intellectual capital. Edvinsson and his team at Skandia were instrumental in publishing the world's first intellectual capital annual report as a one-page section of the company's 1993 annual report. Skandia has divided market value into financial capital and intellectual capital. Intellectual capital is further divided into human capital and structural capital (consisting of customer capital and organizational capital). Organizational capital is then broken down into innovation capital (ultimately consisting of intellectual property and intangible assets) and process capital.[37]

NOTES

1 Luehrman, T.A. (1998) "Strategy as a portfolio of real options," *Harvard Business Review*, **76** (5), p. 89.

2 Mintzberg, H., Ahlstrand, B. & Lampel, J. (1998) *Strategy Safari*, Free Press, London.

3 Mintzberg *et al.* (1998) op cit.

4 Mintzberg *et al.* (1998) op cit.

5 Barwise, P. (1997) "Strategic investment decisions and emergent strategies," *Financial Times Mastering Management*, Financial Times Pitman Publishing, London.

6 Mintzberg, H. (1990) "The manager's job: folklore and fact," *Harvard Business Review*, **68** (2), p. 163.

7 Grove, A.S. (1996) *Only the Paranoid Survive*, p. 128, Currency/ Doubleday, New York.

8 See also Bartlett, C.A. & Ghoshal, S. (1994) "Changing the role of top management: beyond strategy to purpose," *Harvard Business Review*, **72** (6), p. 79.

9 Hamel, G. & Prahalad, C.K. (1989) "Strategic intent," *Harvard Business Review*, May–June.

10 Prahalad, C.K. & Hamel, G. (1990) "The core competence of the corporation," *Harvard Business Review*, **68** (3), p. 79.

11 Rumelt, R.P. (1994) "Foreword," in *Competence-Based Competition* (eds Hamel, G. & Heene, A.), John Wiley & Sons, Chichester.

12 Hamel, G. & Prahalad, C.K. (1994) *Competing for the Future*, Harvard Business School Press, Boston.

13 Rumelt, R.P. (1994) op cit.

14 Hamel, G. (1994) "The concept of core competence," in *Competence-Based Competition* (eds Hamel, G. & Heene, A.), John Wiley & Sons, Chichester.

15 Birchall, D.W. & Tovstiga, G. (2001) "The strategic potential of a firm's knowledge portfolio," in *The Financial Times Handbook of Management* (eds Crainer, S. & Dearlove, D.), Financial Times Prentice Hall, London.

16 http://www.public.itrs.net/home.htm

17 Groenveld, P. (1997) "Roadmapping integrates business and technology," *Research Technology Management*, September–October.

18 Meyer, M.H. & Mugge, P.C. (2001) "Make platform innovation drive enterprise growth," *Research Technology Management*, **44** (1), pp. 25–39.

19 Bain & Company Website – http://resultsbrief.bain.com/june/junresultsbriefBR.htm

20 van der Heijden, K. (1996) *Scenarios: The Art of Strategic Conversation*, Wiley, New York.

21 de Geus, A. (1997) *The Living Company*, Nicholas Brealey Publishing, London.

22 Schoemaker, P. (1995) "Scenario planning: a tool for strategic thinking," *Sloan Management Review*, **36** (2), p. 25.

23 Hamel, G. and Prahalad, C.K. (1994) *Competing for the Future*, Harvard Business School Press, Boston, p. 79.

24 Mintzberg, H. (1994) *The Rise and Fall of Strategic Management*, Free Press, London, p. 375.
25 Islei, G., Lockett, G. & Naude, P. (1999) "Judgemental modelling as an aid to scenario planning and analysis," *Omega*, **27** (1), pp. 61–73.
26 Argyris, C. & Schon, D. (1978) *Organizational Learning*, Addison-Wesley, Reading, MA.
27 Senge, P. (1990) *The Fifth Discipline*, Doubleday/Currency, London.
28 Denton, J. (1998) *Organizational Learning and Effectiveness*, Routledge, London.
29 Huber and others (Pedlar, M., Burgoyne, J. & Boydell, T.) (1997) *The Learning Company: a Strategy for Sustainable Development*, McGraw Hill, London; Senge, P. (1990) *The Fifth Discipline: the Art & Practice of the Learning Organization*, Century Business, London; Huber, G.P. (1991) "Organizational learning: the contributing process and the literatures," *Organization Science*, **2** (1), pp. 88–115.
30 Fiol, C. & Lyles, M. (1985) "Organizational learning," Academy of Management, *The Academy of Management Review*, **10** (4), pp. 803–14.
31 Nonaka, I. (1991) "The knowledge creating company," *Harvard Business Review*, **69** (6), p. 96.
32 Nonaka, I. & Takeuchi, H. (1995) *The Knowledge Creating Company*, Oxford University Press, New York.
33 von Krogh, G., Ichijo, K. & Nonaka, I. (2000) *Enabling Knowledge Creation*, Oxford University Press, Oxford.
34 Sveiby, K.E. (1997) *The New Organizational Wealth*, Berret-Koehler Publishers, Inc., San Francisco.
35 Stewart, T.A. (1997) *Intellectual Capital*, Nicholas Brealey Publishing, London.
36 Edvinsson, L. & Malone M.S. (1997) *Intellectual Capital*, Piatkus, New York.
37 Roos J., Roos G., Edvinsson L., Dragonetti N.C. (1997). *Intellectual Capital*, MacMillan Press Ltd, Basingstoke.

Resources

This chapter provides an excellent overview of references in the literature, books, and Websites that the reader can use to develop a broad understanding of the field.

Seminal books and journal articles on key notions, concepts, and ideas related to future proofing. Many of these references served as resource material for the various sections of this book.

BOOKS

Scenarios and foresight

De Geus, Arie (1997) *The Living Company*, Nicholas Brealey Publishing, London.

Greenwald, C.G. & Rudolph, S.E. (1996) "Scenarios and long-term visioning: critical elements of technology strategy, *Prism*, Second Quarter.

Kleiner, A. (1996) *The Age of Heretics, Heroes, Outlaws and the Forerunners of Corporate Change*, Nicholas Brealey, London. Recounts how the early pioneers developed the practice of scenario planning.

Schwarz, Peter (1991) *The Art of the Long View: Planning for the Future in an Uncertain World*, Doubleday/Currency. Explains how to conduct a scenario exercise.

Shoemaker, Paul J.H. (1992) "How to link strategic vision to core capabilities," *Sloan Management Review*, Fall.

Van der Heijden, Kees (1996) *Scenarios: The Art of Strategic Conversation*, John Wiley & Sons, New York. A useful handbook on the principles of scenario planning.

Technology roadmapping

Goodman, R.A. & Lawless, M.W. (1994) *Technology and Strategy*, Oxford University Press, New York.

Groenveld, Pieter (1997) "Roadmapping integrates business and technology," *Research Technology Management*, September–October.

Quality Matters, special issue on roadmapping, internal Philips publication, no. 73, April (1996).

Willyard, C.H. & McClees, C.W. (1986) "Motorola's technology roadmap process," *Research Management*, September–October.

Quality function deployment

Collins, J.M. & Schwope, A.D. (1994) "Integrated product definition: using QFD for the business of product development," *Prism*, Fourth Quarter.

Hauser, J.R. & Clausings, D. (1996) "The House of Quality," *IEEE Engineering Management Review*, Spring.

Competencies and capabilities

Birchall, David W. & Tovstiga, George (2001) "The strategic potential of a firm's knowledge portfolio," *Financial Times Handbook of Management*, Financial Times Prentice Hall.

Hamel, Gary & Prahalad, C.K. (1989) "Strategic intent," *Harvard Business Review*, May–June.

Hamel, G. (1994) "The concept of core competence," in *Competence-Based Competition* (eds Hamel, G. & Heene, A.), John Wiley & Sons Ltd, Chichester.

Hamel, G. & Heene, A. (1994) *Competence-Based Competition*, John Wiley & Sons, Chichester.

Hamel, Gary & Prahalad, C.K. (1994) *Competing for the Future*, Harvard Business School Press, Boston.

Prahalad, C.K. (1993) "The role of core competencies in the corporation," *Research Technology Management*, November–December.

Prahalad, C.K. & Hamel, Gary (1990) "The core competence of the corporation," *Harvard Business Review*, May–June.

Sanchez, R. & Heene, Aimé (1997) "A competence perspective on strategic learning and knowledge management," in *Strategic Learning and Knowledge Management* (eds Ron Sanchez and Aimé Heene), John Wiley & Sons.

Teece, D. & Pisano, G. (1998) "The dynamic capabilities of firms: an introduction," in *Technology, Organization and Competitiveness* (eds G. Dosi, D.J. Teece & J. Chytry), Oxford University Press.

Knowledge management

Edvinsson, Leif and Malone Michael S. (1997) *Intellectual Capital*, Piatkus, New York

Nonaka, Ikujiro (1991) "The Knowledge Creating Company," *Harvard Business Review*, November–December.

Nonaka, Ikujiro and Takeuchi, Hirotaka. (1995). *The Knowledge Creating Company*, Oxford University Press, New York.

O'Dell, C. & Grayson, C.J. (1998) *If Only We Knew What We Know*, Free Press, New York.

Roos, J., Roos, G., Edvinsson, L., and Dragonetti, N.C. (1997) *Intellectual Capital*, MacMillan Press Ltd, Basingstoke.

Stewart, Thomas A. (1997) *Intellectual Capital*, Nicholas Brealey Publishing, London.

Sveiby, Karl Erik (1997) *The New Organizational Wealth*, Berret-Koehler Publishers, Inc., San Francisco.

von Krogh, G., Ichijo, K. & Nonaka, I. (2000) *Enabling Knowledge Creation*, Oxford University Press, Oxford.

Leonard-Barton, D. (1995) *Wellsprings of Knowledge*, Harvard Business School Press, Boston.

Organizational learning

Argyris, Chris (1991) "Teaching smart people to learn," *Harvard Business Review*, May-June.

Senge, Peter M. (1990) *The Fifth Discipline - The Art and Practice of the Learning Organization*, Doubleday/Currency, London.

Senge, Peter, Kleiner, A., Roberts, C., Ross, R., Roth, G., and Smith, B. (1999) *The Dance of Change*, Doubleday/Currency, New York.

Connectivity, new economy

Davis, Stan and Meyer, Christopher (1998) *Blur - the Speed of Change in the Connected Economy*, Warner Books, Reading, MA.

Evans, Philip E. and Wurster, Thomas S. (1997) "Strategy and the New Economics of Information," *Harvard Business Review*, September-October.

Evans, Philip E. and Wurster, Thomas S. (2000) *Blown to Bits*, Harvard Business School Press, Boston.

Hamel, Gary (2000) *Leading the Revolution*, Harvard Business School Press, Boston.

Kelly, Kevin (1998) *New Rules for the New Economy*, Viking, Harmondsworth.

Moore, James (1996) *The Death of Competition*, John Wiley & Sons.

Shapiro, C. and Varian, H.R. (1999) *Information Rules*, Harvard Business School Press, Boston.

Tapscott, D., Lowy, A., and Ticoll, D. (1998) *Blueprint to the Digital Economy*, McGraw-Hill.

Value proposition

Drucker, Peter F. (1994) "The Theory of Business," *Harvard Business Review* **72** (5), p. 95.

Treacy, M. and Wiersema, Fred (1995) *The Discipline of Market Leaders*, Addison-Wesley Publishing Company.

Technological discontinuities and disruptive technologies

Bower, Joseph L. & Christensen, Clayton M. (1995) "Disruptive Technologies: Catching the Wave," *Harvard Business Review*, January–February.

Christensen, Clayton M. (1997) *The Innovator's Dilemma*, Harvard Business School Press, Boston.

Foster, Richard J. (1986) *Innovation: The Attacker's Advantage*, Summit Books.

Prahalad, C.K. (1998) "Managing Discontinuities: The Emerging Challenges," *Research Technology Management*, May–June.

Strategic management

Mintzberg, H. (1994) *The Rise and Fall of Strategic Management*, Free Press, London.

Mintzberg, H., Ahlstrand, B. & Lampel, J. (1998) *Strategy Safari*, Free Press, London.

Porter, M.E. (1997) "How Competitive Forces Shape Strategy," *Harvard Business Review*, July-August.

Gratton, Lynda (2000) *Living Strategy*, Financial Times Prentice Hall, Harlow.

Organizational change

Christensen, Clayton M. and Overdorf, Michael (2000) "Meeting the Challenge of Disruptive Change," *Harvard Business Review*, March–April.

Imparato, N. and Harari, O. (1996) *Jumping the Curve*, Jossey-Bass Publishers.

Stebel, Paul (1994) "Choosing the Right Change Path," *California Management Review*, Winter.

Strebel, P. (1996) "Why Do Employees Resist Change?" *Harvard Business Review*, May–June.

Strebel, Paul (1998) "Creating Industry Breakpoints: Changing the Rules of the Game," *IEEE Management Review*, Summer.

WWW RESOURCES

The Internet contains a wealth of information related to various aspects of "Future Proofing." The following website references indicate organizations and sites devoted to the various topics related to "Future Proofing"; they provide numerous links to further resources including tools, approaches, conferences, and more related to the subjects.

General

World Future Society (www.wfs.org); a not-for-profit educational and scientific organisation for people interested in how social and technological developments are shaping the future; features a variety of resources including publications, meetings, forecasts, etc.

Foresight

Foresight Institute (www.foresight.org); The Foresight Institute's goal is to guide emerging technologies to improve the human condition. Foresight focuses its efforts upon nanotechnology, the coming ability to build materials and products with atomic precision, and upon systems that will enhance knowledge exchange and critical discussion, thus improving public and private policy decisions.

UK Foresight (www.foresight.gov.uk); The UK's Government-led Foresight program brings people, knowledge, and ideas together to look ahead and prepare for the future; a very comprehensive site with many links to other resources.

UNIDO (www.unido.org); many useful links to technology foresight in Asia, Europe, USA, OECD.

Knowledge and innovation management

Sveiby (www.sveiby.com.au); a site devoted to creating business for knowledge, contains useful insights by Karl Erik Sveiby and links to other resources.

Entovation International (www.entovation.com); a site committed to knowledge and innovation management; includes links to products and services, assessment tools, and other relevant resources; ENTOVATION® International News, and Annual Reviews.

Knowledge Associates (www.knowledgeassociates.com); self-description: "Imagine one place to obtain a Total Knowledge Management Solution embracing education, consulting methods, technology tools, implementation, support, and web hosting services."

MINT (http://mint.mcmaster.ca); the McMaster University (Hamilton, Canada) Management of Innovation and New Technology (MINT)* Research Centre; MINT is a think tank in the field of innovation research; puts out an electronic newletter.

Technology roadmapping

Sandia National Laboratory (www.sandia.gov/Roadmap); good source of information on technology roadmapping including description of process and glossary of terminology.

Scenario planning

Global Business Network (www.gbn.org); a worldwide membership organization, GBN engages in a collaborative exploration of the future, discovering the frontiers of knowledge and creating innovative tools for strategic action.

Siemens FutureScape Team (www.ic.siemens.com); "... a small, interdisciplinary group chartered by executive management to identify long-term megatrends and discontinuities that will influence information and communication technology. FutureScape is committed to viewing 'the world' in new ways that will enable the company to translate visions and opportunities into tomorrow's business."

St. Gallen Center for Future Research (www.sgzz.ch); a Swiss organization working with scenario planning and system dynamics. Most of the Website is in German.

PERIODICALS AND MAGAZINES

Knowledge Management (www.kmmag.co.uk); described as the magazine for the knowledge-enabled enterprise; £40/year.

Fast Company (www.fastcompany.com); described as the magazine for people who make business work; $23.95/year.

Business2.0 and *eCompany* (www.business2.com); describes itself as: "Business 2.0 is the essential tool for navigating today's relentlessly changing marketplace, particularly as it's driven by the Internet and other technologies. It discovers and reports on the smartest, most innovative business practices and the people behind them. It delivers surprising, useful insights, and explains how to put them to work." $19.99/year.

Wired (www.wired.com); describes itself as ". . . the journal of record for the future. Daring. Compelling. Innovative. Courageous. Insightful." $12/year.

Technology Review (www.technologyreview.com); MIT's magazine of Innovation; $34/year (USA); foreign countries add $30.

Making it Work

What would be the value of a concept if it could not be used? This chapter offers specific steps that can be taken to enable a company to future proof effectively.

Future proofing sets out to minimize the risks of investing in organizational capabilities which soon become obsolete and are then prohibitively expensive to reconfigure or dispose of, or to retrain people, even if this is feasible without putting the total business at risk. The overall aim is to find a way forward for the organization which ensures that future obsolescence is minimized by designing so that resources are flexible and open-ended enough to allow for growth, are attentive to the changing needs of stakeholders, and yet are affordable. The focus is on getting a balance between specificity of resources and their flexibility – there is a trade-off to be struck between the lower costs of specificity and the higher costs of flexibility and adaptability.

We assert that foresight methodologies can enable informed strategic formulation and more effective development and deployment of organizational resources to meet a range of possible futures – future proofing. In seeking to establish those areas "at risk" to rapid change, strategies can be developed to minimize the chance of expensive redundancy.

A range of tools can be used in the process of future proofing. The basic process is illustrated in Fig. 10.1.

The starting point to future proofing is the identification of alternative scenarios for the specific unit of analysis of interest, be it a product, service, firm, or industry. In preparation for the scenario exercise, background information should be collected about the business environment and the changes taking place, particularly on the technology front. A number of methods and tools should be considered for application in the process and the many sources of information reviewed.

Foresight studies carried out at industry or national level can be very useful as an input to a scenario exercise. These cover many areas. For example, in the United Kingdom alone there are three thematic panels and 10 sectoral panels studying fields as diverse as crime prevention, chemicals, and health care. Foresight brings together a wide variety of expertise in developing a framework and this then undergoes considerable consultation in order to give an informed opinion about likely directions. It is not normally restricted to technology development but rather takes in the wider economic, political, social, and environmental context of business operations. Many national governments run such programs, so comparison across national boundaries can be

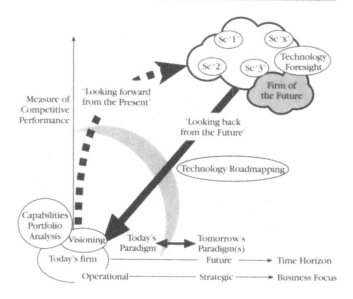

Fig. 10.1 Concepts and techniques for future proofing.

worthwhile. It enables firms to access "expert" opinion in a way which may be infeasible otherwise due to cost and time limitations. These sources are invaluable and freely available to all.

An example of headline outputs from a Foresight initiative is presented in the box below.

HEADLINE OUTPUT FROM A FORESIGHT INITIATIVE

Construction associate program

Many areas are emerging from discussions in which positive action now might bring about significant improvement in the future. The following list includes some of those, and is not meant to be exhaustive but indicative of the discussion and feedback received to date:

1 Construction futures – the UK construction industry needs to make better use of the economic forecasts carried out by the financial community in order to think longer term and more strategically, and as a result react more quickly to changing economic conditions.
2 Construction processes – gain a better understanding of how the formulation and operation of construction industry supply chains might be improved.
3 Health and safety – to reduce the root causes of accidents and to improve the reporting of "near-misses." Possible solutions could be more effective operational education, as well as active consideration of construction methods to identify any activities that are inherently "unsafe," which could be replaced by other techniques.
4 Information and communication technologies (ICT) – the construction industry to work with both software houses and government to deliver the ICT it requires.
5 Materials – how can the construction industry best exploit new materials and components that offer significant advantages such as smart composites, biomimetics, intelligent insulation, eco-friendly adhesives also for sustainability, to recycle and re-use materials?
6 Whole life thinking – improved methods of calculating the "whole life cost" of a facility, taking proper account of the durability of the materials and components used and environmental sustainability needs to combat the potential effects of global warming and depleting natural resources.

Source: http://www.foresight.gov.uk

National, industry, and company-specific technology roadmaps also serve to inform this stage in the overall process of future proofing. These government-sponsored maps are much more specific than Foresight exercises about the likely development of relevant technologies in key business sectors for the national economy and are used to set national and industry targets for R&D development, so these are pre-competitive. Industry roadmaps are also pre-competitive and again can be used to focus long-term R&D and also lead to co-operation among competitors within the industry so as to accelerate development and reduce overall costs. Company-specific roadmaps are clearly not normally intended to be shared publicly, although it is likely that suppliers and customers will be involved in parts of the analysis. Also some of the expertise used in formulating the roadmap will come from universities, research establishments, and consultancies, so it is unlikely that the information will be proprietary, but it is the way in which the business configures the technologies and then develops control and mastery over those areas essential to its future that will give it competitive edge.

Quality function deployment is a useful tool as a preliminary to product or services roadmapping because it emphasizes the position of the customer and customer needs and preferences, and identifies the functional requirements of products. It also takes into consideration the firm's competitive position. The basic elements of the house of quality used in a QFD exercise are shown in Figure 10.2.

The overall aim when future proofing is to achieve a blueprint for action which has been widely "tested" for validity and is widely accepted within the organization and its strategic partnership as an appropriate way forward. In arriving at the blueprint, the models and assumptions underpinning the conceptualization should have been made explicit and been thoroughly tested across a range of experts from a diversity of disciplines and background experiences.

Schoemaker[1] stresses that final scenarios should meet three criteria.

1 They should be different from one another and reflect different futures rather than variations on a theme.
2 They should be relevant and connect to mental maps and users' concerns.
3 They should be internally consistent and make sense in the context of the drivers being examined.

Clearly one important determinant of success at this stage in the process of future proofing is to build robust scenarios. In many ways

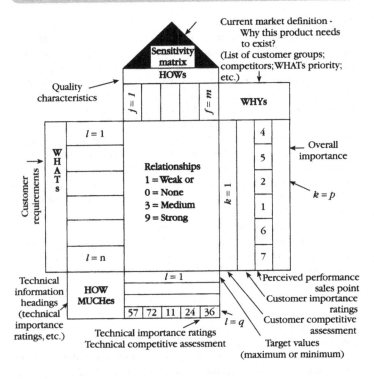

Fig. 10.2 The basic elements of the house of quality.

the scenarios are just the foundation stones for difficult decision making. However, two features will strongly determine long-term success – the quality of inputs into the process and the process itself. This depends on a number of factors relating to inputs, process, and outputs.

INPUTS INTO THE PROCESS – THE COSTS OF DOING IT

The main issues in relation to inputs into the scenario exercise are as follows.

» The quality of the data – its validity, reliability, and currency.
» Recognition of limitations to the analysis – those areas where information is inadequate and residual uncertainties therefore are present in the prognosis.
» The commissioning of research to plug any essential gaps.
» The expertise brought to bear in analysis of the data available – its breadth, depth, and range. The greater the diversity in terms of background – educational and cultural, business experience, outside interests, creativity and analytical skills, and many other facets – the more confidence the outputs will instill.
» The extent to which the "known" is separated from "conjecture" and the mental models underpinning any scenario are made explicit.
» Identification of, consensus on, and categorization of those areas in the analysis where risk and exposure are high ("uncertainties," in Shell's language) and those that are relatively secure and more or less predictable (predetermined elements).

The output from this process should be at least two scenarios, but preferably four. They may well have features in common where elements are predetermined, but they should be distinct in relation to areas of high uncertainty. The scenarios ideally will be in narrative form and will be identified by an unusual name, one which will be recalled easily as the scenarios get embedded into the organization's "storytelling" and will make it easy to remember the essence of each scenario.

PROCESS ISSUES – HOW TO DO IT

The quality of the output is in part dependent on the quality of the input, but at least as important to success is the management of the process. We have already stressed the need to introduce a high degree of diversity of thinking into the activity. This requires considerable preparation and management. There are a number of both strategic and operational issues to consider when planning a process of this type.

1 It is essential that the body responsible for strategic direction takes responsibility for the process.

2 The executives' aims and expectations for the exercise need clarification at the outset. Then a system needs to be agreed for monitoring progress and reviewing those aims on a regular basis.

3 The overall process is complicated and contains many uncertainties. Like any project, it needs careful planning before embarking on the activity. An organizational structure needs to be in place to make it possible to achieve the end product. It has to be clear which groups will be responsible for which elements and which decisions. Those involved in background work such as reviewing national and industry Foresights, scenario development and testing, then developing an overall strategic direction, communications, monitoring, and review, need to be carefully briefed.

4 The scope of the exercise has to be decided at an early stage so that adequate resource planning can be put in place.

5 Targets and timescales need to be agreed at the outset.

6 The total process needs to be considered thoroughly during planning – it is relatively easy to get a group together for a day to quickly develop some scenarios, but is this what the organization actually wants? Unless thought has been given at the outset to how the scenarios are going to be used, and to such issues as who will have access to work with them and in what way, it is unlikely that the exercise will go beyond the theoretical.

7 The process needs dedicated management.

8 The process needs expert facilitation, particularly given the seniority in their profession of many of the participants.

9 A budget needs to be agreed – experts are at a premium and often expect high fees.

10 The logistical aspects of organizing meetings and consultation needs careful thought – facilities have to be conducive to the type of cerebral activity involved.

OUTPUTS FROM THE PROCESS – THE BENEFITS

In addition to the scenarios themselves, there will be a series of outputs from the process overall, including reports and other documentation, so that reference can be made to the outputs and a review undertaken in the future.

1 Filtered information as background for the scenario planning groups.
2 The scenarios themselves along with the detailed work underpinning them, such as mental models and assumptions being made.
3 The results of the analysis of the scenarios in relation to future direction for the business, again with details of assumptions introduced including risk assessments.
4 Detailed reports of the testing of the proposed directions in relation to financial and technical feasibility, organizational capability and fit, as well as social acceptability and the resulting modifications.
5 A documented process with a review of its effectiveness and lessons learned.

An important element is the process of future proofing as a means of supporting the development of the learning organization. This and other intangible benefits should be included in any review. Also, future proofing is not a "once-and-for-all" activity but something which is ongoing. So one important output is a plan for embedding the approach into the organization's functioning and a process for taking it forward.

At the end of the day the organization is seeking to address one of its biggest challenges. It is seeking to move forward in a direction which reflects the best view possible of the future and what it holds. The output should challenge previously held personal views, assumptions, and mental models across the organization and should be capable of sensitizing the organization and galvanizing its members to action. But above all it should incorporate the principles of future proofing and provide sufficient flexibility in thinking and action to ensure that the organization does not get caught out by disruptive changes, particularly those due to technological advances.

NOTES

1 Schoemaker, P. (1995) "Scenario planning: a tool for strategic thinking," *Sloan Management Review*, **36** (2), p. 25.

Frequently Asked Questions (FAQs)

Q1: What is future proofing?

A: See Chapter 2, ''Future proofing'' and Chapter 8.

Q2: How is future proofing carried out?

A: See Chapter 6, ''Key issues and current debate.''

Q3: Is it reliable?

A: See Chapter 10.

Q4: How can it be used by business?

A: See Chapter 7.

Q5: Who should do it?

A: See Chapter 8.

Q6: What's the cost of doing it?

A: See Chapter 6, ''Technology roadmapping/QFD.''

Q7: What's the benefit?

A: See Chapter 6, ''Technology roadmapping/QFD'' and ''Scenario planning.''

Q8: How long does it take?

A: See Chapter 6, ''Scenario planning.''

Q9: How often do you have to do it?

A: See Chapter 6, ''Technology roadmapping/QFD'' and ''Scenario planning.''

Q10: What tools and resources do I need?

A: See Chapter 2: ''Risk assessment and portfolio management,'' ''Trends analysis,'' Chapter 6, ''Capabilities portfolio analysis,'' Chapter 8, ''Organizational learning – key concepts and thought leaders,'' Chapter 10, Table 10.1.

Acknowledgments

There are a number of colleagues we would like to thank for their help and support in researching and writing *Future Proofing*.

First of all we would like to thank Margy Smith for her untiring help with the preparation of the manuscript. We would thank Raj Kumar for the development of one of the case studies, and Foong Wing Keong for supplying the materials for another based on experiences in Malaysia. We would also like to thank Dr Friedrich Pinnekamp (ABB Group R&D and Technology) and Mr Wylie Rogers (ABB Corporate Communications) for providing background information for the ABB case study. We also thank Nigel Spinks for the interest shown and his help with key references.

In addition, we would like to thank the following authors for their kind permission to reproduce diagrams and tables:

Groenveld, P. (1997) "Roadmapping integrates business and technology," *Research Technology Management*, Sept/Oct. pp. 48-55, Figures 6 and 7.

Kauffman, P., Ricks Wendell, R., Shockcor, J. (1999) "Research portfolio analysis is using extensions of quality function deployment," *Engineering Management Journal*, **11** (2), pp. 3-9, Exhibits 1, 3, 4 and 5.

Koen, P.A. (1997) "Technology maps: choosing the right path," *Engineering Management Journal*, December, pp. 7-11, Exhibit 5.

Partovi, F. (1999) "A quality function deployment approach to strategic capital budgeting," *The Engineering Economist*, **44** (3), pp. 239–260, Figure 4.

Prasad, B. (1998) "Review of QFD and related deployment techniques," *Journal of Manufacturing Systems*, **17** (3), pp. 221–234, Figure 3.

Finally we would like to thank those, too numerous to name, to whom we owe a debt for their inspiration and also their leading edge thinking. However, we take full responsibility for manuscript preparation and hope that we have not misrepresented or diluted their thinking. We have also endeavored to reference materials throughout the book which provide access to sources of use to any reader wishing to gain a deeper understanding of the underlying concepts and practice.

Index